NM

Studies on Themes and Motifs in Literature

Horst S. Daemmrich
General Editor

Vol. 41

PETER LANG
New York • Washington, D.C./Baltimore • Boston
Bern • Frankfurt am Main • Berlin • Vienna • Paris

Space and Time
on the Magic Mountain

Hugo G. Walter

Space and Time
on the Magic Mountain

Studies in Nineteenth-
and Early-Twentieth-Century
European Literature

PETER LANG
New York • Washington, D.C./Baltimore • Boston
Bern • Frankfurt am Main • Berlin • Vienna • Paris

Library of Congress Cataloging-in-Publication Data

Walter, Hugo.
Space and time on the magic mountain: studies in nineteenth and early
twentieth century European literature / Hugo G. Walter.
p. cm. — (Studies on themes and motifs in literature; vol. 41)
Includes bibliographical references and index.
1. European literature—19th century—History and criticism. 2. European
literature—20th century—History and criticism. I. Title. II. Series.
PN761.W35 809'.894'09034—dc21 97-52156
ISBN 0-8204-3994-0
ISSN 1056-3970

Die Deutsche Bibliothek-CIP-Einheitsaufnahme

Walter, Hugo:
Space and time on the magic mountain: studies in nineteenth
and early twentieth century European literature / Hugo G. Walter.
−New York; Washington, D.C./Baltimore; Boston; Bern;
Frankfurt am Main; Berlin; Vienna; Paris: Lang.
(Studies on themes and motifs in literature; Vol. 41)
ISBN 0-8204-3994-0

The paper in this book meets the guidelines for permanence and durability
of the Committee on Production Guidelines for Book Longevity
of the Council of Library Resources.

Printed in the United States of America.

This work is dedicated to my mother,
Elli R. Walter.

chical) and physical (organic) behavior and aberrations. Mann's protagonist ultimately exemplifies the Nietzschean strategy of Zarathustran self-overcoming in the attempt to develop and enrich the intellectual vitality of the self.

Castorp develops a diastolic sense of time (a sense of the fluidity and openendedness of time) on the magic mountain in the world of the Berghof Sanatorium which becomes a hermetic sense of time upon his departure at the end of the novel to participate in the world war. He also shows a diastolic sense of space, especially in the section entitled "Snow," where he experiences the aura of an endless landscape. In contrast to Wordsworth's persona who achieves a diastolic sense of time through a diastolic sense of space (that is, space precedes time), Mann's protagonist attains a diastolic sense of space after developing an expansive sense of time (that is, time precedes space).

For Mann's protagonist the magic mountain is a threshold space at the fragile edge of time and eternity, life and death, the beautiful and the sublime. As for Hilton, so for Mann the mountain environment is a place of intellectual vitality but without the same motivation. Hilton's Shangri-La aims to preserve the cultural heritage of human civilization in anticipation of a future international cataclysm. Mann's Berghof Sanatorium offers intellectual stimulation not only as a diversion from the pervasive aura of decay and death but also as a foundation for the emotional, intellectual, and spiritual expansion of the self in its attempt to cultivate a more insightful understanding of humanity.

The interest in mountains as inspirational and sublime places may be traced back to biblical times. C. E. Macartney asserts in *Mountains and Mountain Men* the importance of mountains in biblical literature: "Mountains dominate the history of the Bible and the divine revelation. . . . Great events in the history of redemption, and in the lives of the great personalities of the Bible are associated with the mountains of Bible lands" (5). Macartney proceeds to describe the significance of various mountains of biblical lands:

> On a mountain the ark rested after the Flood, when God showed mercy to mankind. . . . On Mount Sinai the Ten Commandments were given to Moses. On Mount Carmel the prophet Elijah overcame the prophets of Baal. . . . On Mount Calvary Christ died for our sins, and on Mount Olivet he ascended up into heaven. (5)

The mountain in the Bible was also a place of prayer and meditation, of reflection on the self, the world, and the interaction between the two. The mountain in the Bible and throughout world literature is

I will show that Hilton's protagonist affirms a Bergsonian life-philosophy (especially the notion of being able to create time freely from the present moment onward) in his quest for a sense of continuity with the world of Shangri-La. I will also show that Hilton's conception of Shangri-La is influenced by and similar to the sense of light, silence, and atmosphere of American luminist painting of the nineteenth century.

For Hilton the mountain is a place of cultural and intellectual vitality infused with a profound serenity. As for Wordsworth, the mountain experience for Hilton is most vital and stimulating when it is conceived of as a threshold experience at the interface of life and death, time and eternity. Unlike Wordsworth's mountain experience, which is characterized by an expansion of the self, Hilton's is motivated by a preservation of the self, especially against the belligerent mentality of the early twentieth century and in response to the destructiveness of the first world war and its consequences.

Like Arnold's persona in "Stanzas from the Grande Chartreuse" Hilton's protagonist ultimately adopts a hermetic approach in his quest for the magic mountain. The novel ends with the protagonist's attempt to return to the magic mountain which he has left too abruptly—in his awareness of the seemingly inevitable differentiation of Shangri-La and the world of everyday mortality Conway realizes that he still has much to learn from the intellectual serenity and spatial and temporal vitality of Shangri-La. For Shangri-La represents a response of profound wisdom to the seemingly unalterable penchant of civilization for destruction and violence—it is a sanctuary of cultured peace which may shape a more humanitarian future.

In the final chapter I will discuss the conception of time and space in Thomas Mann's *The Magic Mountain*. *The Magic Mountain* is the story of a young engineering student who, before the beginning of his apprenticeship in a Hamburg shipbuilding firm, decides to spend a few weeks visiting his cousin in an Alpine tuberculosis sanatorium and never returns, realizing instead his affinity for such an environment of death and attaining a vital sense of intellectual and spiritual fulfillment in this threshold realm of life and death permeated by disease and decay. *The Magic Mountain* reveals the significant influence of Schopenhauer, Nietzsche, and Freud on Mann, representing a confluence of such themes as the notion of the union of genius and suffering, especially in an artistic figure, whether literal or symbolic, the Dionysian power of music, and the relation between mental (psy-

"Stanzas from the Grande Chartreuse," the culminating presentation of the magic mountain experience in Arnold, offers an adventure as physically isolated as that of Mann's or Hilton's magic mountain. The persona's strategy in Arnold's poem is hermetic, finding emotional security away from the world of everyday mortality. Although the persona finds at least a symbolic affirmation of his emotional vitality in this secluded, non-secular environment, the Grande Chartreuse is not a pervasively congenial place.

For Arnold's persona is not stimulated by the monastic culture as Conway is in *Lost Horizon* by the culture of Shangri-La. Rather, Arnold's persona remains in this isolated spot less because it comforts him vitally than because it allows him to escape the world, permeated on the one hand by the industrial and social problems of Victorian society and the accompanying sense of despair in the face of such problems and on the other by the dubious sense of progress offered by Macaulay's interpretation of history. Arnold's persona is content to find a temporary sanctuary until he has begun to revitalize his soul in the spirit of lines 91–96:

> Oh, hide me in your gloom profound,
> Ye solemn seats of holy pain!
> Take me, cowl'd forms and fence me round,
> Till I posses my soul again;
> Till free my thoughts before me roll,
> Not chafed by hourly false control!

In chapter three I will examine the understanding of space and time on the magic mountain in James Hilton's *Lost Horizon*. This novel articulates a relatively timeless world—the world of Shangri-La—which is almost inaccessible, which one finds only by chance or fate. The Tibetan monastery which lures Conway, the protagonist, from the migratory life of consular service is a seemingly timeless world of subtly vital life at the fragile edge of eternity. Conway, intuitively interested in finding a relatively timeless space of intellectual, emotional, and spiritual vitality, develops a diastolic conception of time (a sense of the openendedness of time) in transforming a diastolic to an hermetic sense of space. What is unique about Conway's hermetic sense of space is that it is expansive and magnanimous in its inwardness— the aura of this space is dynamic, not static, it is pervaded by an underlying motion that floats down to the valley and soars up to the heights of the mountain and the heavens.

an expansiveness of space. Moreover the majestic intellect can converse with the spiritual world as well as with past, present, and future generations of humankind until time shall be no more.

I will show that Wordsworth's magic mountain experience is influenced and informed, both positively and negatively, by the potential and social context and consequences of the French Revolution. Wordsworth's persona ultimately aspires to achieve a sense of expansiveness of the mind and spirit which asserts a sense of liberation from the vicissitudes of everyday mortality, especially from the destructive, violent tendencies of the contemporary world, and affirms an experience of totality with the natural environment and with the spatial and temporal parameters of such an environment. For Wordsworth, this is not an escape, but rather an experience of revitalization which will re-energize not only the creative self but also his belief in the "heart of man" (13.241) as the theme of his work.

In chapter two I will discuss the awareness of time and space on the magic mountain in several of Matthew Arnold's poems, "Resignation," "Stanzas in Memory of the Author of 'Obermann'," "Empedocles on Etna," and "Stanzas from the Grande Chartreuse." Arnold's magic mountain experience is a quest for a profoundly serene wisdom beyond the frailties and miseries of commercial, industrial Victorian England.

Arnold's "Stanzas in Memory of the Author of 'Obermann'" describes the poet as being perpetually torn between two impulses, between the urge to experience the world and the inclination to solitude. Arnold's persona wishes to be one of those who have gained the wisdom to be in the world but not of it, who approach the world with active concern and critical detachment. In "Stanzas" the persona leaves the magic mountain in despair, caught between an "unstrung will" (183) and a "broken heart" (183), unable to resolve the tension within himself. This tension, which has a Derridean aura to it in its sense of determining and then unraveling meaning or in its assertion of the fluidity or instability of meaning, affirms the threshold nature of the magic mountain experience at the interface of time and eternity.

In "Empedocles on Etna" Arnold reinforces and intensifies the despair of the creative persona who cannot resolve his inner tension, his desire to be part of the world and his inclination to differentiate himself from it, and who cannot find a congenial place in the world, a place characterized by at least a semblance of the tranquillity of Obermann's alpine solitudes.

Acknowledgements

I would like to thank the following professors for their encouragement, guidance, supportiveness, and thoughtfulness during the past few years: Robert Ready, John Warner, Janet Burstein, Sara Henry-Corrington, James Pain, Michael Ryan, and David Kohn of Drew University and Jack Becker and Richard Kopp of Fairleigh Dickinson University.

I would also like to thank Professor Horst Daemmrich of the University of Pennsylvania and Dr. Heidi Burns of Peter Lang Publishing, Inc. for their insightful and thoughtful comments regarding my manuscript.

Finally, I would like to thank Lisa Dillon of Peter Lang Publishing, Inc. for her helpful assistance and patience in the production of the manuscript.

I would like to thank the following institutions for permission to reprint from the following works:

The Prelude, by William Wordsworth, edited by Jonathan Wordsworth, et al. © 1979, W. W. Norton & Company, New York, NY, reprinted with the permission of the publisher.

Tintern Abbey and *Ode: Intimations of Immortality* by William Wordsworth from *English Romantic Writers* by David Perkins, copyright © 1967, Harcourt Brace & Company, reprinted by permission of the publisher.

Victorian Poetry and Poetics, Second Edition, by Walter E. Houghton and G. Robert Stange. © 1959, 1968, Houghton Mifflin Company, reprinted with the permission of the publisher.

Lost Horizon, by James Hilton © 1933, 1936, William Morrow & Company, Inc., reprinted with the permission of the publisher.

The Magic Mountain, by Thomas Mann, translated by H. T. Lowe-Porter. © 1927, 1955, Alfred A Knopf, Inc. and Random House UK, reprinted with the permission of the publishers.

The Inner Reaches of Outer Space, by Joseph Campbell. © 1986, Harper & Row, Publishers, Inc., reprinted with permission of the publisher.

Table of Contents

Introduction

M. H. Nicolson in *Mountain Gloom and Mountain Glory* sees the experience of the mountain ambience in literature as signifying either mountain gloom or mountain glory. She argues that through the mid-eighteenth century mountains were typically characterized as places of gloom and described in conventional terms. During the latter part of the eighteenth century and especially during the Romantic period of the late eighteenth and early nineteenth century the notion of mountain gloom was transformed into mountain glory and mountains were portrayed in a new, more vital language (Nicolson 21).

There is another type of mountain experience, which I would like to call the quest for the magic mountain (using Thomas Mann's phrase from his novel of the same name). The magic mountain, typically an environment aesthetically and intellectually distinct and physically isolated from the material world of everyday reality, is a threshold realm of life and death, at the interface of life and death, time and eternity, where the protagonist goes to achieve an epiphanic moment of awareness, to revitalize himself, and to develop a sense of time and space.

In contrast to Nicolson's characterization of the mountain experience in literature as pervaded either by gloom or glory, the quest for the magic mountain is primarily a threshold experience, an experience of intensely felt creative vitality at the threshold of life and death. It is at this threshold of life and death, time and eternity, that the protagonist of the mountain experience is inspired to develop a distinctive sense or philosophy of time and space which is intimately related to his self-revitalization, and to his epiphanic moment of awareness.

The protagonist in the magic mountain experience may try to conquer time, to change it, to reshape it, to eliminate it, to measure it, to mask it, or even to coexist in a complementary relation with it. He may try to expand space, to enclose it, to transform it, or even to reaffirm or redefine himself through it. Whatever philosophy of time and space the protagonist of each of the literary worlds discussed below adopts, develops, and strengthens (and he may even re-evaluate and modify his philosophy of time and space in the course of his experience) in his quest, such an individual inevitably evolves the same kind of Promethean devotion to his task that Rilke speaks of as being essential to the genuine artist who consecrates himself to his work.

In this series of essays I will discuss the conceptions of time and space developed by the protagonists in several magic mountain experiences in nineteenth- and early-twentieth-century European literature. Each of the magic mountain experiences will be considered in its historical context, although some of the experiences are more historically determined than others. I will focus on several magic mountain experiences in selected works of William Wordsworth, Matthew Arnold, James Hilton, and Thomas Mann.

In the first chapter I will consider Wordsworth's conception of time and space developed in his magic mountain experience on Mt. Snowdon. I will trace Wordsworth's quest for the magic mountain from "Tintern Abbey" through the "Ode: Intimations of Immortality" to the culminating scenario in *The Prelude*. On Mt. Snowdon in *The Prelude* Wordsworth's persona realizes and participates in the expansiveness of time and space and envisions the end of time and mortality. This experience of time is similar to Georges Poulet's notion of the Romantic self participating in a time of experienced continuity. But it goes beyond Poulet's idea of continuity as a "living and thinking experience solely because by an uninterrupted motion the mind unifies in a moving line the diverse temporal elements of a self-same existence" (29). For Wordsworth's persona in *The Prelude* aspires to achieve a sense of totality with nature, a diffusion and a reaffirmation of the magnanimity of the creative self in the expansiveness of the natural environment.

In Book 14 of *The Prelude*, for example, Wordsworth's persona speaks of the capacity of the "majestic intellect" (14.67) to participate in and shape the expansiveness of space and time. In representing "the emblem of a mind / That feeds upon infinity" (14.70–71), the majestic intellect reveals its potential to participate in an expansiveness of time. In dealing with the "whole compass of the universe" (14.92) in such a way that it can "send abroad / Kindred mutations" (14.93–94), the majestic intellect shows its capacity to participate in such a place of contemplation as well as a space to create or receive an epiphanic revelation. The moments which an individual sensitive to the nuances and subtleties of his environment spends on the mountain are sacred moments, which often seem timeless—these are moments where, as Rousseau says, "time counts for nothing, where the present lasts forever."

Such moments of revelation are comparable to Joyce's notion of epiphany as a sudden spiritual manifestation. Of the idea of epiphany, Morris Beja writes in *Epiphany in the Modern Novel* that it is one kind of moment "of illumination, and the main tradition of such moments begins on the road to Damascus with Paul" (24). Beja continues to argue that while the prophets had visions of God and visitations from Heaven, these were "not the same sort of sudden enlightenment that has since been called the conversion experience" (24).

In the Renaissance as well there are significant images of mountains and descriptions of mountain experiences in art and literature. For example, Petrarch's "Ascent of Mont Ventoux" (written in the mid-fourteenth century) offers an experience of intellectual and spiritual growth which is generated and strengthened by a mountain adventure. Initially in this essay Petrarch speaks of the hardship of climbing the mountain, though such a climb strengthens the soul. When he reaches the summit, Petrarch, standing in a daze, experiences a sense of expanded space in the sweep of the view that spreads out before him. Then he shifts his thoughts to a consideration of time, contemplating the changes that mortality has brought to his own life and character.

As he is about to leave the summit with the emergence of evening, Petrarch looks into a copy of St. Augustine's *Confessions* that he carries with him. The passage that he finds reminds him of the supreme importance of the soul in contrast to material things. He is subsequently inspired to consider himself in the tradition of spiritual awareness of St. Anthony and St. Augustine and to acknowledge how superior the range of human contemplation is in contrast to the mountain. Petrarch concludes this section in an affirmation of the strategy of mountain gloom by asserting that we should strive not to stand on mountain-tops, but to strengthen our souls against earthly desires. In the transformation of the original challenge of climbing the mountain to the challenge of refining and strengthening the soul, the mountain itself has been diminished in stature and almost reduced to an image of human conception without an innately significant existence.

   More than a century later Leonardo da Vinci uses mountain imagery more positively and more dynamically than Petrarch. In several of
Leonardo's paintings, including *The Virgin of the Rocks* (1483–85)
and the *Mona Lisa* (1503–07), mountains or mountainous terrain
(consistently images of mountain glory) signify an integral part of the
work.

   In *The Virgin of the Rocks*, for example, the aura of the rocks, and
especially of the more mountainous rocks in the background of the
painting, complements and reaffirms the semantic focus—the etherial
light which emanates from the madonna and child bathes the mountainous rocks in the foreground as well.

   In the *Mona Lisa* Leonardo uses rocks and mountainous crags less
as formal and thematic complements than as supplemental features in
relation to the central figure. Though the figure and the landscape
share a similarly darkened coloring, the face and neck of the Mona
Lisa are the most highly illuminated aspects of the painting. If the
Mona Lisa may be said to reveal a melancholy awareness of the fragility of life, then the fleeting forms of the mountains in the background
reaffirm such an awareness.

   In *Virgin and Child with St. Anne* (1508–10) the mountains play
an even more prominent role, sharing not only some of the color of
the drapery in the foreground, but also melting gradually into the arrangement of figures.

   In Leonardo's work, then, the image of the mountain (though never
the primary focus) is intimately connected to the formal and semantic
focus of the painting in which it occurs, whether through a shared
color pattern with the figure or figures in the foreground or through
its structural prominence. The expansiveness of space and time implied in the mountain imagery of Leonardo's paintings is seen as well
in some of the works of Joachim Patenier, who was one of the first
landscape painters to depict mountains as a vital dimension of the
natural environment and of the vision of nature.

   The notion of the capacity of the self, especially the creatively vital
self, to participate in the expansiveness of space and time may be
seen especially in eighteenth-century theories of the imagination and
the sublime. E. L Tuveson has observed that in such theories "the
contemplation of a physically vast object, or one suggesting vastness,
somehow increases the physical extent of the mind" (105).

   John Baillie in *An Essay on the Sublime* (1747) asserts similarly
that "every Person upon seeing a grand object is affected with some-

thing which as it were extends his very Being, and expands it to a kind of Immensity" (4). Baillie goes on to suggest that the soul is elevated in viewing the heavens and expanded in considering extended natural prospects. Joseph Priestly (1777) affirms this sense of the potential expansiveness of the soul in his statement: "The mind . . . conforming and adopting itself to the objects to which its attention is engaged, must enlarge itself to conceive a great object" (151). Alexander Gerard suggests in *An Essay on Taste* (1780) that "we always contemplate objects and ideas with a disposition similar to their nature. When a large object is presented, the mind expands itself to the extent of that object, and is filled with one grand sensation" (12).

Albert Wlecke in *Wordsworth and the Sublime* argues that, in considering these conceptions of spatial extension, one should not "take literally these metaphors of the expanding space of mind" (51), for "they are intended to describe not the nature of the mind but the experience of consciousness when consciousness is directed towards the 'larger Scenes and more extended Prospects' of nature" (51). In this experience of sublime consciousness "insofar as the mind is felt to expand, it is sensed as possessing an increasing amount of extension, as spreading itself outward into space" (52). This sense of an expansive consciousness is in the spirit of Longinus, for whom the sublime represented an uplifting of the soul in contemplation of the majestic or the magnificent.

In *Analytical Inquiry into the Principles of Taste* Richard Payne Knight discusses the theory of the sublime of Longinus:

> All sublime feelings are, according to Longinus, feelings of exultation and expansion of the mind, tending to rapture and enthusiasm; and whether they be excited by sympathy with external objects, or arise from the internal speculations of the mind, they are still of the same nature. In grasping at infinity the mind exercises the powers . . . of multiplying without end; and, in so doing, it expands and exalts itself, by which means its feelings and sentiments become sublime. (36)

Such a "grasping at infinity" is precisely what Wordsworth's majestic intellect of *The Prelude* and the personae or protagonists in Arnold, Hilton, and Mann do in expanding the self.

Thomas Gray, in describing his experience in the mountainous European landscape, also speaks of seeing spirits at noon and sensing the presence of death perpetually before his eyes. The following passage exemplifies Gray's sense of the mountain adventure as a threshold experience between life and death:

It is six miles to the top; the road runs winding up it, commonly not six feet
broad; on the one hand is the rock, with woods of pine-trees hanging overhead; on the other, a monstrous precipice, almost perpendicular, at the bottom of which rolls a torrent. (62)

Gray's depiction of the mountain experience as signifying the fragile
edge of life and death anticipates the mountain experience of
Wordsworth, Arnold, Hilton, and Mann, all of whom portray the sublime ascent and sometimes terrifying descent as an interaction and
fusion of gloom and glory.

Friedrich Schiller in the poem "Der Spaziergang" finds emotional,
aesthetic, and intellectual solace and rejuvenation in the presence of
the mountain "mit dem rötlich strahlenden Gipfel" (1). For Schiller,
the experience of the "magic mountain" as an existential condition at
the threshold of life and death generates the artistic vision of the
poem which encompasses, as does the dream-vision of Castorp in
Mann's *The Magic Mountain*, the constructive, positive evolution of
the human spirit as well as its destructive aspects. The threshold nature of such a sublime experience as the encounter with the magic
mountain is reinforced in Schiller's essay *Concerning the Sublime*
(*Über das Erhabene*, 1801) where he asserts that the feeling of the
sublime is a mixed feeling combining antithetical, contradictory emo-
tions. In "Der Spaziergang" Schiller's "Ich" resolves the metaphysical
tensions of the "magic mountain" experience through his revitalization in the purifying presence of nature and through his awareness of
participating in the eternal cyclicality of the natural world.

Andrew Wilton in *Turner and the Sublime* asserts that Kant "jus-
tifies Burke's association of pain with the sublime by arguing that
there is a 'painful' discrepancy between the capacity of the reason to
estimate the magnitude of an external phenomenon, and the capacity
of the imagination to represent it" (29). Burke's sense of the sublime,
which is in the tradition of the Aristotelian notion that fear is central to
the experience of tragedy, contrasts with that of R. P. Knight, who
sees in the sublime experience only expressions of passion and expansive mental energy without the presence of fear.

In *Philosophical Enquiry into the Origin of Our Ideas of the
Sublime and the Beautiful* Edmund Burke defines the sublime as
follows:

Whatever is fitted in any sort to excite the ideas of pain and danger, that is to
say, whatever is in any sort terrible, or is conversant about terrible objects

. . . is a source of the sublime; that is, it is productive of the strongest emotion which the mind is capable of feeling. (13)

The Burkean sublime is an integral part of the mountain experience of
all the major personae and protagonists of the literary works discussed
in this essay and is especially important for those in Arnold's
"Empedocles on Etna" and "Stanzas from the Grande Chartreuse"
and in Mann's *The Magic Mountain*.

Yet, even in Book 14 of *The Prelude* one might find traces of the
Burkean sublime. Wordsworth's majestic intellect, in signifying "the
emblem of a mind / That feeds upon infinity, that broods / Over the
dark abyss" (70–72), seems to participate in the terrible silence and
majestic solitude of which Burke speaks. R. P. Knight claims that such
silence and solitude may be sublime "by partaking of infinity" (363)
and by representing an expansion of mind, for the mind "in expanding itself, will of course conceive grand and sublime ideas, if the imagination be in any degree susceptible of grandeur and sublimity" (363).
Knight's comments are especially interesting because they affirm the
importance of the expansion of the mind in the experience of sublimity and because they assert that it is the privilege and responsibility of
the perceiving and conceiving subject to create and shape the substance and vision of infinity.

Wordsworth's persona, the majestic intellect of *The Prelude*, affirms the significance of infinity to inspire his aesthetic, intellectual,
and spiritual development while at the same time asserting that he has
the capacity to participate in a sense of infinity, even in the shaping of
infinity, by his communicating with past, present, and future generations until "Time shall be no more" (111). Hans Castorp, too, in Mann's
The Magic Mountain, experiences infinity and the expansiveness of
infinity in the "Snow" episode when he has the dynamic visionary
conception amidst the majestic solitude of the mountain snow.

The awareness of the potential expansiveness of time and space
and of the sublime in a mountain landscape was prominent in the
visual arts of the time as well, whether in the works of Salvator Rosa,
J. M. W. Turner, J. R. Cozens, Joseph Wright, or P. J. de Loutherbourg,
among others. One of Turner's earliest significant compositions of
such a mountain environment, *Buttermere Lake* (1798), is described
by Wilton as follows:

The dark sides of the mountains rise into turbulent vapors around the faintly
gleaming lake, which partially reflects light from the obscured sky and the arc

of a brilliant rainbow that spans half the composition. Beneath its arch lies a
flat alluvial valley dotted with buildings, also reflecting light. Beyond, a som-
bre mountain heaves itself up into the clouds. (35)

Turner printed with the title in the catalogue a few verses taken
from Thomson's "Spring":

Till in the western sky the downward sun
Looks out effulgent—The rapid radiance instantaneous strikes
The illumin'd mountains—in a yellow mist
Bestriding earth-the grand etherial bow
Shoots up immense, and every hue unfolds.
(88–9, 191–92, 193, 203–04)

Wilton writes that these lines, which were chosen by Turner to accom-
pany his painting, confirm that Turner's aim "was to create an image
conveying a sublime natural effect—an effect involving 'effulgence,'
'grandeur,' and 'immensity,' among other ideas mentioned in
Thomson's lines" (36).

Such images and ideas as "effulgence," "grandeur," and "immensity" are essential features of the mountain experiences of the literary
personae and protagonists discussed in this book. The mountain will
be a source of illumination, an inspirational radiance which not only
suggests an expansiveness of space and time, but also stimulates the
emotional and intellectual vitality of the personae at the threshold of
life and death. Thomson's sense of the grandeur and immensity of the
mountain landscape is affirmed in "Summer" of *The Seasons*, where
the airy vision of one mountain image leads to another implying an
expansiveness of space and time, linked to the distant horizon and to
a feeling of a profound immensity of shade.

A similar mountain adventure is presented in the Earl of Shaftesbury's
The Moralists: A Philosophical Rhapsody (1709), in which individuals attain a new and vital vision of the world in a threshold experience
on a mountain at the edge of the abyss. Shaftesbury's protagonists
find "a Nature, superabundant, diverse, various, evidence of a God of
plentitude who creates all possible varieties of experience" (Nicolson
293). Such a sense of the expansiveness and infinity of spatial and
temporal possibilities in the universe is found and revitalized in the
nineteenth century, especially in the Romantics, and in the twentieth
century in such works as Hilton's *Lost Horizon* and Mann's *The Magic
Mountain*. Edward Young's *Night Thoughts* (1742–45) shares
Shaftesbury's belief in the possibility of infinite space and infinite time

and extends Shaftesbury's notion by asserting the complementarity of a profundity of space, a depth of time, and powerful creativity.

Karl Kroeber in *Romantic Landscape Vision*, after suggesting that Thomson's *The Seasons* prepares the way for new kinds of interaction between artists and natural phenomena, writes that the potentialities of such new interrelations "are first realized in Wordsworth's vision from Mt. Snowdon in the final book of *The Prelude*. Wordsworth's description is of weather, especially of clouds, but it is intensely localized (Wales, Snowdon, Bethkelet's huts) as Thomson's views never are" (101–02).

Kroeber goes on to claim that the Snowdon episode is appropriately placed at the end of *The Prelude*: "Snowdon climactically affirms the capability of imagination to identify man's place in nature" (102). Kroeber stresses that the progress of *The Prelude* represents a growth in imaginative development which involves a concomitant emphasis on, or fusion of, sight and sound. Such an organically developing consciousness is intimately involved in the process of self-renewal which affirms the dynamic continuity of a self that intuitively believes in the importance of a spatial and temporal expansiveness.

Chapter 1

William Wordsworth

In *William Wordsworth: A Life* Stephen Gill writes that "Tintern Abbey" (written in 1798) is Wordsworth's "hymn of thanksgiving" (120) for the "energies in the natural order that make for unity, which enable man to know himself part of the great whole of the active universe" (129–30). Wordsworth's persona (the "I" in the poem) overcomes the fragmentation of the self that occurs in "Yew-tree Lines" by appreciating profoundly the "sense sublime / Of something far more deeply interfused" (95–96) which inspires him to see in nature the emotional, spiritual source of his experience of a diastolic, expansive sense of space and time. In "Tintern Abbey" Wordsworth reveals a diastolic sense of space and a sense of time that is both hermetic and orphic, hermetic in the sense that the persona is more aware of mortality, orphic in the sense that the persona believes intuitively that any expansiveness of space may lead to a feeling of expanding time.

The importance of a sense of space is stressed from the beginning of "Tintern Abbey." In the first ten to fifteen lines Wordsworth speaks of the significance of the "steep and lofty cliffs" (5) which not only inspire profound thoughts, but also represent the link between the earth and "the quiet of the sky" (8). The aura of heavenly tranquillity is subsequently applied to the repose which the persona experiences under the dark sycamore. Wordsworth views with admiration various features of his immediate natural environment, "the plots of cottage-ground" (11), "the orchard-tufts" (11), and "the hedge-rows" (15). He asserts that though he has not seen "these beauteous forms" (22) directly for several years, these images of nature have influenced his mind and heart powerfully from a distance. These images have given him not only "sensations sweet" (27), but they have also infused his soul with a semblance of the tranquillity which characterizes "the quiet of the sky" (8).

The sensitive contemplation of "these beauteous forms" (22) creates the "serene and blessed mood" (41) in which the individual experiences a psychic suspension of corporeal existence and becomes a living soul. In attaining this existential condition the persona prepares himself (as lines 46–48 suggest) to achieve a diastolic sense of space and time. At this epiphanic moment of harmony and joy the persona sees "into the life of things" (49). This vision or visionary capacity seems to be a precursor of and perhaps even comparable to the "faith that looks through death" (185) of the Immortality Ode.

In the next section of the poem starting with line 49 the persona claims that he has often turned to the sense and spirit of the "sylvan Wye" (56) and its surroundings to help and guide him through his present existence. The sense of spatial fluidity which was established in the first fifteen lines of the poem is reinforced by the image of the "sylvan Wye" (56) wandering through the forest. Though the Wye represents an image of water not of earth (in contrast to the previously foregrounded images of nature) all of the dominant features of nature described so far in the poem possess an inner energy. The "orchard-tufts" (11) and "hedge-rows" (15), like the "sylvan Wye" (56), are infused with a dynamic motion which affirms the vitality of nature and perhaps even enhances the capacity of the living soul to see into the life of things.

The return to this inspirational place is important not only for the present revitalization of the individual, but also for his future development. Although the persona is able to revive some of the past spirit of this space and of his feeling for nature, he realizes the difference between his earlier and his current experience of nature. The emotional passion which the persona felt as a youth in the presence of nature has been toned down to a more serene awareness of and feeling for nature. Yet, there is still a unity of past and present through the power of memory which sustains and will continue to preserve the poet's faith in the vitality of the present. Moreover, change is not seen necessarily as a negative dimension of life; rather, it produces "abundant recompense" (88), perhaps most of all in the increasing development of a more mature and insightful creative vision.

The persona, in becoming a more mature and profound observer of and participant in nature, feels a presence that disturbs him "with the joy / of elevated thoughts" (94–95). This "sense sublime" (95) is characterized above all by a spatial expansiveness—the motion and the spirit which the persona senses as the source of nature's creative energy and sublimity is a diastolic spatiality that encompasses not only sky, earth, and water, but also the mind of man.

Wordsworth's persona asserts that because he feels vitally this spatially generated energy which "impels / All thinking things" (100–01) and "rolls through all things" (102) he is a nature-lover, a lover of the spatial expansiveness of nature. This awareness of the diastolic power of nature inspires the persona to proclaim that nature (and the language of the sense) represents the guide and guardian of his heart, soul, and moral being.

Line 97 offers one example of the power of the diastolic spatiality of nature to influence significant dimensions of the surrounding world. In line 97 the persona perceives, or perhaps conceives of, time in terms of space. In suggesting that the dwelling of this presence in nature is "the light of setting suns" (97), the persona implies the transcendence of time through space. The phrase "setting suns" (97) suggests a series or succession of evenings which are unified in the spatially motivated aura of their light. This emphasis on space as the defining quality of this experience of the presence of nature, exemplified by the use of the image "dwelling" (97), is reinforced by the following phrases, "round ocean" (98), "living air" (98), and "blue sky" (99), all of which are spatially vital and spatially motivated images.

The "sense sublime / Of something far more deeply interfused" (95–96), which is fulfilled in the conception of a motion or a spirit pervading nature, has already been presented in the poem prior to line 95. For the description of the "orchard-tufts" (11) losing themselves "'Mid groves and copses" (14), the "hedge-rows" (15) running wild, and the sylvan Wye wandering through the woods are all examples of the "motion" (100) and "spirit" (100) which rolls through all things. The potential for diastolic spatiality is perhaps even implied in the first few lines of the poem where the persona speaks of hearing the waters "rolling from their mountain-springs" (3), implying his capacity to envision an existential vitality beyond the immediate natural space. The persona's capacity for experiencing and participating in, as well as creating, a spatial expansiveness is affirmed in the ensuing lines in his perception of the cliffs connecting the landscape with the quiet of the sky.

The spatial metaphor is reaffirmed in the last section of the poem, lines 112–159, where the persona speaks for example of the importance of the mind, which through the benevolent and pervasive influence of nature "shall be a mansion for all lovely forms" (140) and of the significance of the memory which shall "be as a dwelling-place / For all sweet sounds and harmonies" (141–42). The structural framework of this spatial metaphor reinforces the sense of space established by the initial experience of the sycamore. The poet grounds or establishes himself in a particular space from where he envisions the beauteous forms of nature and the motion and spirit that vitalizes those forms. From this secure, or seemingly secure, space the persona perceives and conceives the diastolic spatiality of his natural environment.

Helen Vendler in "'Tintern Abbey': Two Assaults" asserts the importance of the "continuing force of various paradigmatic identity roles proferred by lyric to centuries of readers" (185). The continuity of the Wordsworthian "I" can be maintained without seeing it as "factually mimetic of its own historical moment of social experience" (185). Vendler is responding to Levinson's argument that Wordsworth has suppressed facts about the description of Tintern Abbey and its environment in a strategy of historical denial as well as to "Barrell's insistence that Wordsworth must have endorsed a connection between gender and language because some of his contemporaries did" (183) by saying that both are "examples of a misplaced historicizing of lyric" (183).

Vendler proceeds to say: "If Wordsworth's aim in 'Tintern Abbey' is, as I believe, to write in longer form 'My heart leaps up,' then he is constructing a geometrical figure for the ego over time, connected by lines between four points" (184). Vendler proceeds to say that if "these are the four different immersions in the landscape that generate the poem, nothing could be more irrelevant to them than the industrialism and the vagrant-haunted Abbey" (184–85). The Wordsworthian "I" can attain a sense of continuity in his own landscape vision, in his own context of emotional, intellectual, and spiritual vitality, which may include, but is not necessarily determined by, the historical experiences which occur simultaneously.

Vendler suggests that the change in the way the word "nature" is used in the poem, especially in the shift from the unpersonified presence of nature meaning "the natural world" in the second part to the personification of nature as female in the third part "was enabled by the entrance of the thought of the speaker's sister, who becomes the genius loci" (187).

Whether or not one argues that the maturation of "wild ecstasies" (138) into "a sober pleasure" (139) parallels or represents a transformation of time and space, it is the aura of spatial expansiveness which possesses and reveals dynamic healing qualities. Only the individual who is aware of and sensitive to the beauteous forms of nature and who develops a profound feeling for nature may achieve this sense of a spatial expansiveness of the soul.

Moreover, only such an individual who loves, admires, and reveres nature may experience a continuity of self by participating in a series of epiphanic moments in which nature so influences the mind and impresses the soul with quietness and beauty that it cannot be adversely affected by the harsh, unsympathetic world of everyday mortality. The highest and most vital condition of mortal existence is signified by a continuity of self in the spirit of the epigraph of the Immortality Ode: "And I could wish my days to be / Bound each to each by natural piety."

The sense of continuity is enhanced by Wordsworth's belief in the presences or Presence of nature. Perkins in *English Romantic Writers* says that for Wordsworth (especially for the Wordsworth of *The Prelude* but manifest through his work) "in the natural world there is not simply a congeries of objects but a Consciousness, a pervading Being, or . . . a Presence" (172). Wordsworth's awareness of continuity—his assertion of the importance of achieving a continuity of self—is connected to and reinforced by his philosophy of organicism. As the universe is a living, dynamically growing and maturing whole, so the self aims to develop organically by encompassing a series of "selves," or moments of existence of the self, in a perpetually self-generating unified vision. However, sometimes the unified vision falls apart and fragments into countermoments of "sightings," not vision.

It is noteworthy that Wordsworth uses the "light of setting suns" to motivate his awareness of a vital presence, a divinely powerful presence, in nature. One might ask why he does not speak of rising suns, suggesting directly an aura of beginnings and renewal. Perhaps one might argue that it is at this threshold moment of evening, of the interface of day and night, and symbolically of life and death, that the persona feels he may most vitally or even exclusively experience the spatial expansiveness of nature. Through his awareness of the spatial expansiveness of nature the persona experiences an expansiveness, spatial and ultimately temporal, of the creative self as powerful as the holistic vitality of the self in Samuel Palmer's painting *Cornfield by Moonlight with the Evening Star* (1827) and in John Constable's *The Hay Wain* (1821).

Wordsworth's Immortality Ode (written 1802–04) is about beauty, the beauty of nature, and creative vitality, and how to make life enjoyable and pleasurable, if not inspirational, when that beauty begins to fade and when that creative vitality begins to diminish. One might also say that Wordsworth's poem deals with an eternal challenge to the human spirit—how to make life meaningful and worthwhile in a world that is fragile and mortal.

For Wordsworth the answer to this challenge, the inspiration to overcome this challenge, is to be found in the following: 1) in Nature, in the eternal, cyclical beauty and dynamism of the natural environment and in the poet's experience of an emotional and a spiritual unity and continuity with that environment; 2) in his own creative capacity as a poet, in his artistic vitality as a creator, which is strengthened as he matures and grows older; 3) in the importance of memory, in the remembrance of significant past personal events which are congenial enough to provide strength and confidence to confront the present and the future; and 4) in the importance of an emotional vitality, of a generous and magnanimous heart and spirit that would include in its perception and vision all aspects of the world (not only fountains, meadows, brooks, and clouds, but also the most inconspicuous flower).

Wordsworth's Immortality Ode begins with a lament about the inevitable passage of time. The first two stanzas reveal a sense of beauty in nature as well as an awareness of mortality, that these beautiful things will pass away. The third stanza reinforces the persona's awareness of mortality and suggests that mortality may be transcended, if only temporarily, by the emotional-spiritual participation of the sensitive individual in the spatial magnanimity and permanence of nature. Although the beautiful in nature may pass away, there is a continuity, a cyclicality in the natural world which overcomes and intensifies the transience of its enchanted moments. The persona will also be revitalized by perceiving the joyousness and vernal vitality of nature.

The fourth stanza affirms initially the joyous aura of nature. In his capacity to appreciate the beauty of nature emotionally and spiritually, the persona enhances his own sense of bliss. Yet, in the midst of the beauty and vitality of nature the persona senses the inevitable flux of time which will ultimately bring about a change in his visionary power. The persona feels a sense of bliss, but is compelled by the subtle signs of mortality to wonder about the fading of the visionary gleam. As in the first two stanzas, the perception of the vital beauty of nature is linked to and challenged by an awareness of mortality, of the flux of time.

The isolated tree, the single field, and the pansy remind the persona of the transience of all animate creatures. The joyousness of the persona has been reduced by the end of the fourth stanza to two interrelated questions: "Whither is fled the visionary gleam? / Where is it now, the glory and the dream?" (56–57). In the first question the "I" seems to raise a concern about his own visionary capacity, as if such a capacity were adversely affected by the presence of images of transience. The second question intensifies the concern of the first. The intensification is made all the more poignant not only by the coupling of the two lines in end-rhyme, but also by the fact that the word "gleam" (56) seems to have energized the formation of "glory" (57) and "dream" (57) in the following line. The concern about the visionary capacity of the persona is transient, for the visionary gleam is revitalized in the last stanzas of the poem, especially in the capability to appreciate a continuity of "spots of time" to make life meaningful.

Stanza five of the Immortality Ode glorifies the time of youth: "Heaven lies about us in our infancy" (66). The child is depicted as being closer to nature emotionally and spiritually. He is closer to the pulse of nature, perhaps because of his pristine imagination and his capacity for wonder. One might think of Ruskin's statement that the genius is largely a child at heart, preserving a capacity for perpetual wonder. The youth is sustained by "the vision splendid" (73) of the beauty of nature—as long as he keeps the spirit of nature in his heart, he will be able to counter the vicissitudes of mortality. In the final two lines of stanza five Wordsworth's persona acknowledges that adulthood is not typically capable of sustaining the profoundly vital visions of youth which ultimately "fade into the light of common day" (76).

In stanza six Wordsworth suggests that nature, realizing the inevitable loss of emotional innocence and fall from a paradisical state of creative grace of "her Inmate Man" (82), produces "pleasures of her own" (77) to encourage the individual conscious of mortality to reflect less upon or to forget the glories of the past. Nature tries to exhort such an individual to believe in the present, in the fullness of nature's vitality in the present, in the spirit of the Augustinian trilogy of the Eternal Present.

Augustine described past, present, and future not only as experiences relating to external space, but also as experiences within the mind of man: "Perhaps it might be said rightly that there are three times: a time present of things past; a time present of things present; and a time present of things future. For these three do coexist some-how in the soul" (324).

Stanza seven reveals Wordsworth's reflections on and thoughts about childhood and the creative urges developing at that time. Wordsworth's persona implies an ingenuous, even profoundly naive, creative capac-ity as the first stage. The child learns through time, with the generous assistance of time, to fulfill the different and inevitable roles or stages of human development. There seems to be an implication here that the persona, because he is cognizant of the generous assistance of time, cannot view time harshly—instead, the persona considers the negative dimension or facet of time, mortality, as inimical and hostile.

Perhaps the capacity to differentiate time and mortality is related to the acceptance of Harold Bloom in *The Visionary Company* of Wordsworth's belief in the potential for unity between mind and na-ture in the "autonomy of the poet's creative imagination" (79). Such a powerful union of vital reciprocity redeems the world of everyday real-ity and intimates, at least symbolically, an immortality of imaginative experience.

Stanza eight continues the apotheosis of youth unaffected by the rapacious flux of time. In his ingenuous creativity and profound sim-plicity the child is a philosopher and prophet who is intuitively aware of the truths which nature's "Inmate Man" (82) strives all his life to find. Like the Romantic painter John Constable, Wordsworth believes in the importance of the permanences of nature and the glory of child-hood to encourage and inspire us and to give us a sense of continuity and transcendence, if only temporary, over mortality.

Wordsworth's persona is poignantly aware of the ultimate power of mortality in stanza eight:

> Thou little Child, yet glorious in the might
> Of heaven-born freedom on thy being's height,
> Why with such earnest pains dost thou provoke
> The years to bring the inevitable yoke,
> Thus blindly with thy blessedness at strife? (121–25)

In suggesting that the child provokes the passage of time, Wordsworth's persona seems to diminish the power of time, and by implication, the destructive presence of mortality. There is a heroic quality to this child who appears, in the spirit of Carlyle's hero in the essay *Heroes and Hero-Worship*, to live in the inward sphere of things and to understand, if only intuitively, the divine idea of the universe. And yet, the use of the word "blindly" (125) implies that the child is unaware, perhaps because he is a "best Philosopher" (110) and "Mighty Prophet" (114) of time, that time cannot flow without his presence. It is note-worthy that the child is described as "glorious" (121) in a spatial con-text, in the freedom of the spirit which spatial magnanimity confers, perhaps to offset the inevitable flux of time.

With respect to the theme of mortality in the Immortality Ode Cleanth Brooks asserts in *The Well Wrought Urn* that we must be aware of the importance of daylight, of sunlight. The climax of the process which is initiated in stanza two by the glorious birth of sun-light is the sunlight, "the light of common day" (76), of stanza five which "has here become the symbol for the prosaic and the common and the mortal" (223). Yet, there is another type of light in the poem which is revealed in the "innocent brightness of a new-born Day" (194). Although perhaps not as eternally radiant as the light in Bernini's *Ecstasy of St. Theresa*, this light of "innocent brightness" (194) illu-minates the inner heart, the soul of softly ecstatic tenderness.

In stanza nine Wordsworth's persona glorifies "those first affec-tions" (148) which represent the sources of our creative and visionary capacity. Moreover, such affections, such "shadowy recollections" (149), have the power to transform the boisterous flux of mortality into epiphanically serene moments of eternal truth. By achieving a conti-nuity of such dynamic moments, the creative self shapes a meaning-ful, vital life. The conception of eternity expressed in this stanza by Wordsworth's persona anticipates that of Hesse's Steppenwolf, who claims that "eternity was nothing else than the redemption of time, its return to innocence, so to speak, and its transformation again into space" (176). For Wordsworth, too, mortality is redeemed in the eter-nity of spatial permanences of pristine vitality.

The persona praises not only those "first affections" (148), which, like "spots of time," will illuminate and guide the rest of his life, but also the "obstinate questionings" (141) of his intellectual curiosity and the "High instincts" (146) which allow for the possibility of transcen-dence. A further development of "High instincts" is the visionary power of the persona at the end of stanza nine who can not only see the "immortal sea" (163), but who can also participate in the presence of the shore of eternity.

In stanza five Wordsworth privileges the early stages of human de-velopment as being closer (or seeming to be closer) to heaven and to the divine—and yet, it is only through the passage of time, which takes us away from that child-like state of innocence and involves a sense of loss, that we can evolve a series of "spots of time" to be the perpetual "fountain-light of all our day" (151) and to make life worthwhile. Of this sense of loss necessitated by transience Durrant writes in *Wordsworth and the Great System.*

> The neo-Platonic notion of the world as a prison-house has served only to provide a provisional account of the loss of the primal joy of childhood. When the loss of that joy has been acknowledged and accepted, what remains is not the consolation of eternal life in a transcendental world, but a strong assertion that the world can be transformed and given life and meaning by the eye of experience—that innocence is not the only basis for that joy. (122)

In articulating in the last stanzas of the Immortality Ode his vision of the eternal permanences of nature and of epiphanic moments of experience which may be reinforced and strengthened by participation in such eternal permanences, Wordsworth's persona intensifies the validity of the introductory three lines: "The Child is father of the Man; / And I could wish my days to be / Bound each to each by natural piety." By striving for a vital sense of continuity, by aspiring to achieve a strategy of continuity which emulates the eternal continuity of nature, Wordsworth's persona asserts that he has the potential to bind his days in a perpetually congenial association of natural piety.

Wordsworth's universe of temporal discourse and his quest for a sense of timeless recurrence are articulated in a language of exuberant spatiality. The permanences of nature provide a sense of joy. John Beer in *Wordsworth in Time* wonders whether Wordsworth's Immortality Ode is an Ode to Joy or an Ode to Nature:

> If Wordsworth had been called to the unwelcome task of identifying his purposes more closely, he would no doubt have been forced to say rather that he was invoking those elements in nature which gave evidence of joy. By addressing the happy shepherd-boys and the creatures of the spring, and by beginning even his last group of stiller natural presences with the word 'Fountains,' he is paying tribute to those unobtrusive vital forces in nature which keep alive the spirit of joy in the human observer. (111)

In stanza ten the persona wishes once again to revel in the effusive dynamism of nature—yet, this is not an ingenuous activity, but rather one infused with an awareness of mortality, an awareness informed and shaped by assiduously "obstinate questionings" (141). Unlike the earlier phase of the persona in stanza three who overcomes his thought of grief merely by expressing it and exhorting the "Child of Joy" (34) to shout merrily to distance any morose or mournful thoughts, the persona of stanza ten admits a poignant awareness of mortality. By this point in the development of the poem such an awareness of the inevitable passing of animate life no longer links with grief. The persona has achieved an emotional and intellectual acceptance not only of the necessity or inevitability of mortality, but also of his capacity to participate in the dynamic cyclicality of nature to transform or transcend such transience.

In the last lines of the stanza the persona responds to his poignant awareness of mortality by asserting that he will find hope and strength in what remains behind after the splendor of the past is gone:

> We will grieve not, rather find
> Strength in what remains behind;
> In the primal sympathy
> Which having been must ever be;
> In the soothing thoughts that spring
> Out of human suffering;
> In the faith that looks through death,
> In years that bring the philosophic mind. (179–86)

Is not what the persona finds in the present as powerful as or even more powerful than what he experienced in the past? He will find strength in a "timeless" present of things past, things present, and things future. In fusing these qualities in the "faith that looks through death" (185), the persona implies his capacity to participate in and to shape an expansive sense of time.

In stanza ten especially Wordsworth's persona attains intimations of immortality not only through the joy of nature, by participating instinctively and vitally in the eternal beauty and dynamic joyousness of nature, but also through his experience of the primal sympathy and the philosophic mind and through his own creativity. In articulating the notion of "the primal sympathy," the poet implies that he is an integral part of the harmonious whole which is the universe. He uses the language of that universe (tangible objects, specific aspects of nature) to describe his place in it and even to suggest a sense of transcendence. We might call Wordsworth an organo-centric poet—in other words, whatever he chooses to describe or present is a whole, not a part. Even when he is describing a part of this universe, for example, the brooks or the clouds, he has the whole in mind. The "soothing thoughts" of this stanza signify not only the poem itself, but also

Wordsworth's creativity as an artist. The philosophic mind represents the mature understanding of Nature linked to the visionary sense of faith which is analogous to the "faith in life endless, the sustaining thought / Of human Being, Eternity, and God" (*The Prelude*, 14.204–05). Wordsworth anticipates here the prospect of a perpetually vital future for humanity as eternal as that of God or a divine force in the universe.

The tone of these lines, and indeed of the entire Immortality Ode, reminds one of the tone of praise, hope, and faith despite mortality and suffering which emerges so strongly in Rilke's *Sonnets to Orpheus*.

Wordsworth and Rilke both celebrate the importance of nature for the creative self and believe in the supreme vitality of eternal silences of truth. Wordsworth speaks in stanza nine of the eternal Silence which nurtures and stimulates "truths that wake / To perish never" (155–56). In Sonnet 1,X to Orpheus Rilke presents a similarly vital silence of eternal resonance:

> There rose a tree. O pure transcendency!
> O Orpheus singing! O tall tree in the ear!
> And all was silent. Yet even in the silence
> new beginning, beckoning, change went on. (17)

In Sonnet 2,XXI to Orpheus the poet exhorts himself to sing of incomparable gardens which he only knows intuitively, gardens which symbolize not only the aesthetic richness of creative vitality but also the tapestry of life. This sonnet is, like the Immortality Ode, a Promethean paean to the eternal permanence of beautiful natural space which may soothe and inspire the persona, and to feeling, to the importance of an orphically vital feeling which revels in the mysteries of life and appreciates the lyrical beauty of everyday existence.

At the end of the Immortality Ode Wordsworth's persona claims that he now loves the brooks even more than when he appreciated them in a state of emotional, intellectual innocence. Though he has gained a lyrical and a philosophical knowledge of the human condition, in conjunction with the melancholy and profound reflectiveness such knowledge is often infused with and inseparable from, he can still appreciate "the innocent brightness of a new-born Day" (194). The final image of nature in the poem is, perhaps not surprisingly (especially considering the importance of "the light of setting suns" from "Tintern Abbey"), an image of evening, which heightens the awareness of mortality. Yet the light of the setting sun in Wordsworth's

Immortality Ode seems as radiantly bright as the light in Van Gogh's *Sower with Setting Sun* (1888).

For what Wordsworth's persona has learned by the end of the poem, expressed so effectively in lines 6 and 7 of the last stanza, is that he has come to appreciate and love Nature even more through his mortality, through his awareness of the inevitable flux of time and animate life, than he did in his earlier, child-like, immortal state. Only through the passage of time which takes us away and displaces us from that child-like state can we develop a series of "spots of time" (as described in stanza nine) to make life meaningful and worthwhile. And it is only through the passage of time that Wordsworth's persona can achieve a mature understanding and vision of Nature. Such a mature understanding and vision of nature involves realizing the importance of the spatial permanences of nature. By believing in and participating in the eternal cyclicality of the spatial permanences of nature which may result in a sensation of "innocent brightness" or in "Thoughts that do often lie too deep for tears" (203) the persona may achieve a dynamic continuity of self and nature and a sense of the expansiveness of space and time.

In achieving a continuity of self Wordsworth's persona in *The Prelude* (1850 version) attains a diastolic sense of time. The persona who can converse with past, present, and future generations of humankind is the one who fulfills the challenge and the promise of the introductory lines of the Immortality Ode. Not only has this persona bound his days together in a continuity of natural piety, but he has transcended the sense of the existence of days by asserting that he envisions the end of time.

The importance of continuity is emphasized throughout *The Prelude*. In Book 14, for example, the persona speaks of the capacity of higher minds to approach the universe in a magnanimous spirit of inquiry and sensitivity. They have the potential to emanate from themselves "kindred mutations" (14.94). Through communicating with a series of kindred mutations, which are revelations and elaborations of the creative self, the persona achieves a dynamic continuity of self.

Robert Langbaum suggests in *The Mysteries of Identity* that whereas Hume considers continuity a fiction, for Wordsworth "continuity is the fundamental reality" (29). Langbaum proceeds to claim that "for Wordsworth, Keats and the other romanticists, continuity is dynamic" (29). It is such a continuity of growth which allows us to absorb "individual perceptions into an intuited whole" (29). Through this dynamic sense of continuity Wordsworth's "majestic intellect" (14.67) is ultimately able to encompass diverse "spots of time" into a vibrant, organically developing whole.

The crucial difference between the strategy of the personae with respect to the theme of continuity in the Immortality Ode and in *The Prelude* is marked by a shift from a relatively passive to a consistently active tone. In the Immortality Ode the persona wishes that his days could be bound to each other by natural piety. In *The Prelude* the persona signifies the higher mind which creates and shapes its own continuity of existence.

Harold Bloom writes that "the Nature of *The Prelude* is what Wordsworth was to become, a great teacher" (5). He proceeds to say that Nature is so powerful a teacher "that it must first teach itself the lesson of restraint, to convert its immediacy into a presence only lest it overpower its human receiver" (5). Through the inspirational mediating presence of nature Wordsworth's persona will achieve not only a dynamic continuity of self but also a unified, visionary "majestic intellect" (14.67).

Mary Jacobus in "Apostrophe and Lyric Voice in *The Prelude*" says that "the poet himself, Wordsworth implies, is not only murmurous but has inward ears that can hear; this is what makes him a poet" (156). Jacobus goes on to say that "imagined sound becomes a way to repress or deny writing and undo death. If a monument marks the site of a grave, voice—'breathings for incommunicable powers'—gives evidence of a poet's enduring life" (156). Such a powerfully vital creative persona not only sees "the emblem of a mind / That feeds upon infinity" (14.70–71) but also hears "its voices issuing forth to silent light / In one continuous stream" (14.73–74).

For Jacobus visionary power is a heightened sense of hearing which makes language into "something ghostly, nonreferential, ancient, and without origin, like the homeless voice of waters in the Snowdon episode" (156). This power of hearing is an integral aspect of the majestic intellect who would converse with the spiritual world in an aura of timeless voices.

The aspiration to achieve a vital continuity of self begins with the concern to attain a dynamic and an open-ended sense of space. For only when the persona has gained a powerful sense of space can he devote himself to the quest for a continuity of self and the concomitant diastolic sense of time. The importance of this sense of space appears already at the beginning of *The Prelude*. In the first ten to fifteen lines of Book 1 the persona asserts the significance for his own emotional, aesthetic, and intellectual vitality of an open sense of space which encompasses multiple dimensions of nature. Not only does the persona describe himself as being "free as a bird to settle where I will" (1.9), but he proclaims that the earth is before him, that he may participate in any spatial aura of nature which innately attracts him.

Having liberated himself from the city where he remained "a discontented sojourner" (1.8), the persona suggests that the renewed sense of diastolic space which he experiences allows him to breathe again. The intensity of the language the persona uses to describe his feeling for the spaciousness of nature and the contrast between the liberation of self in nature as opposed to the limitation of self in the city implies that the persona's experience of a sense of space is crucial to his existence.

Once he has asserted the importance of space the persona introduces the element of time into his language, speaking of "long months of peace" (1.24) and "long months of ease" (1.26). Yet, at this initial stage of the work the temporal is less an independent entity than an outgrowth of or supplement to the spatial. Time is conceived of in terms of space—for the persona says that the long months of peace are his in prospect, which is a spatial construction.

The potential continuity of the self is developed and enhanced throughout *The Prelude* by the sense of continuity of the self and nature. In Book 1, for example, the persona speaks of feeling not only the breath of heaven blowing on his body, but also a correspondent breeze within the self, which, though seemingly tempestuous, is essential to activating the creative energy of the self.

As the opening book of *The Prelude* progresses, the persona affirms the importance of space by saying that he poured out his soul to the open fields. In this ambience of diastolic space the persona realizes the importance not only of spontaneous expression, but also of the capacity of nature to revitalize the self. The open sense of space is defined and strengthened by the existence of spacial places, each a locus amoenus, which generate the aesthetic and spiritual power of the natural space. One such distinctive space is the "green shady place" (1.62) or "the sheltered and the sheltering grove" (1.69) which the persona discovers. The renovating power of this experience of nature is enhanced by its being characterized by an aura of perfect stillness.

Wordsworth's quest for the liberation of the self from the spirit, but not the substance, of everyday mortality derives its philosophical foundation from several eighteenth-century notions of the imagination which assert the capacity of the creatively vital self to participate in the expansiveness of time and space.

For example, John Baillie in his *An Essay on the Sublime* asserts that "every Person upon seeing a grand object is affected with something which as it were extends his very Being, and expands it to a kind of Immensity" (4). Baillie goes on to suggest that the soul is elevated in viewing the heavens and expanded in considering extended natural prospects. Joseph Priestly affirms this sense of the potential expansiveness of the soul in his statement: "The mind . . . conforming and adopting itself to the objects to which its attention is engaged, must as it were, enlarge itself, to conceive a great object" (151). Alexander Gerard, in his *An Essay on Taste*, suggests that "we always contemplate objects and ideas with a disposition similar to their nature. When a large object is presented, the mind expands itself to the extent of that object, and is filled with one grand sensation" (12).

Friedrich Schiller in *On the Sublime* (*Vom Erhabenen*, 1793) addresses the issue of the sublime object in his distinction between the practically-sublime in which we feel our existence to be threatened and the theoretically-sublime which challenges primarily our conditions of knowledge. Schiller reinforces the distinction as follows:

> An object is theoretically-sublime insofar as it brings with it the notion of infinity, something the imagination does not feel itself capable of depicting. An object is practically sublime insofar as it brings with it the notion of a danger that we do not feel ourselves capable of overcoming with our physical powers. (24–25)

Albert Wlecke in *Wordsworth and the Sublime* argues that, in considering such conceptions of spatial extension, one should not "take literally these metaphors of the expanding space of mind" (51), for "they are intended to describe not the nature of the mind but the experience of consciousness when consciousness is directed towards the 'larger Scenes and more extended Prospects' of nature" (51). In this experience of sublime consciousness "insofar as the mind is felt to expand, it is sensed as possessing an increasing amount of extension, as spreading itself outward into space" (52).

The possibility of unifying mind and nature becomes clear, suggests Wlecke, "if we remember that the extension of the mind throughout space tends to become infinite insofar as the 'grand Object,' to which consciousness is struggling to accommodate its capacity, is in itself unbounded" (52). Wlecke proceeds to make the interesting point that the mind, in confronting sublimity, may become lost: "It almost seems as if the very intensity of the sense of the spatialization of the mind carries within itself a potential sense of a kind of 'aspatiality,' of passing over into a dimension of being where no localization of the self is possible" (53).

Wlecke distinguishes between Cartesian space (the extension of which allows for the determination and localization of the object) and sublime space (the space that is produced by the mind's sense of itself expanding outward with the concomitant potential for the indetermination and dislocation of the subject) to suggest that when the sense of dislocation becomes too strong, the subject moves towards a sense of transport or transcendence. This point is similar to Hartman's claim that Wordsworth's expansive imagination exposes him to the terrors of "apocalypse," to the possibility of the destruction and loss of his world. To counter this potential Wordsworth, suggests Wlecke, aims to "lodge his mind in nature's phenomena" to conserve the world and to localize a consciousness that will ultimately tend towards a sense of transport (54).

To challenge further the anguish and intensity of the dislocating experience the persona may suggest an identity or unity of creator and created in a higher state of consciousness. The belief in a sublime consciousness becomes a continuation of some eighteenth-century notions of divinity, positing the mind as a creating divinity. This uplifting of the soul in contemplation of the majestic or magnificent, in the spirit of Longinus, culminates in an extension of the sublime consciousness, in an expansion of the mind and its own powers.

This quest for an openness of space is intimately linked not only to the emotional and spiritual regeneration of the persona but also to the preservation and revitalization of his creative faculties. In Book 1 the persona says that the serenity he experiences becomes a longing to be active which is further transformed to a desire to endow some airy phantasies with outward life. Although the persona admits that he struggles to write because of internal and external impediments (interestingly enough, the external ones are presented in the language of time), he asserts as well an implicit confidence in his creative capacity. In saying that he has a vital soul the persona prepares the way for his ultimate claim in Book 14 that he represents not only "a mind sustained / By recognitions of transcendent power" (14.74–75), but also one that can create kindred mutations and "hold fit converse with the spiritual world" (14.108).

The tension between space and time at this stage of the work is illustrated also in this contemplation about creative vitality. When speaking of the lofty and variegated story which he would like to create, the persona says that the sun, symbol of warmth and regeneration as well as of time's fluidity, brightens and melts its unsubstantial structure. This ultimately negative aspect of time contrasts in the same passage with the security and stability which a sense of space offers, signified in the lines "With meditations passionate from deep / Recesses in man's heart, immortal verse" (1.231–32). The linkage of space, of the space of an inner expansiveness of self, and immortality prefigures the ultimate conception of a diastolic sense of space and a diastolic sense of time.

Despite the importance of space at this point of the narrative, the persona feels listless and unproductive. Yet, he believes that he was early in life chosen to be a creator, that the voices and images of nature were directed, at least partially, at him, that he was selected (perhaps by the divinity in nature) to be a sensitive interpreter of nature. The restlessness of the poetic persona is soothed by his remembrance of the forestate of calm which he had gleaned from nature, which had permeated his soul in the presence of nature. The calm "That Nature breathes among the hills and groves" (1.281) is orphic, not hermetic—it is an outward-directed tranquillity which parallels and reinforces the openness of space.

In Book 1 Wordsworth (aware of the sense of duality in the early self, represented by the simultaneous presence of beauty and fear) proceeds to assert an awareness of mortality in the lines "dust as we were" (1.340) coupled with a sense that the immortal spirit within reveals and strengthens an aura of harmony, that the immortal spirit within the creatively vital self may reconcile discordant elements in a dynamic fusion.

In Book 1 the persona stresses his quest for boundaries, especially for "the horizon's utmost boundary" (1.371). Lines 376–380 seem to suggest, the motion of the boat notwithstanding, that the persona shows the power of this visionary imagination here. It is as if he senses the presence of the huge peak behind the summit of the craggy ridge. Nature seems to be alive, it is a living thing which responds to the presence of Wordsworth's persona. This notion is intensified when Wordsworth speaks of the soul of Nature as the wisdom and spirit of the universe. Nature has inspired the persona to strive beyond "the mean and vulgar works of man" (1.408) and to aspire to be a part of the "enduring things" (1.409), in the process of which the elements of feeling and thought are purified and the persona is encouraged to sense "A grandeur in the beatings of the heart" (1.414).

Book 1 offers a considerable foreshadowing of Book 14. In describing his adventure with the little boat in Book 1, Wordsworth presents elements which are essential to the central visionary experience of Book 14—the moon with its wide swath of light, the mountain and its aura of majesty, and the tension between the limitation and expansiveness of space in nature. One might perhaps view the incident in Book 1 as a challenge to the poetic persona which he will eventually confront more vitally and overcome in the final book. Wordsworth's early awareness of the presences (or Presences) of nature influencing his childhood thoughts and feelings ensures that the constraint of Book 1 will ultimately be transcended. This is partially due to the fact that the congenial birth-place of Wordsworth allowed him to experience early in life an expansiveness of space.

The intensity of Wordsworth's feeling for nature as a child is exemplified by the passage when he speaks of holding "unconscious intercourse with beauty / Old as creation" (1.562–63). The persona feels a deep emotional pleasure in the beauty of nature. Moreover, this sense of nature is not spatially fixed or grounded. In describing "the silver wreaths / Of curling mist" (1.564–65) and the interaction of water and clouds, the persona implies a dynamic fluidity in nature (a Turneresque fluidity) which affirms the expansiveness of nature. In defining his vision of nature with images that rise and soar, Wordsworth suggests that his relation to nature is characterized by an innately dynamic expansiveness of space.

In Book 2 Wordsworth reinforces the sense of space which was developed in Book 1. He describes, for example, the temple or holy scene which has the hermetically orphic aura expressed by the sonnet "Nuns Fret Not." The essential feature of such a place is its tranquillity as well as the "safeguard for repose" (2.114) which it provides.

Wordsworth also speaks of his growing affection for the sun, not only as the magnanimous light of life, but also as a light of expansive spatiality. The image of the sun spreads "His beauty on the morning hills" (2.184) as well as touching the western mountains—this presents the sun as a signifier of diastolic spatiality. The persona, by perceiving the sun's capacity, participates in this expansive spatiality as well. The sun represents a sense of continuity with which the persona wants to infuse his own life.

One of the ways in which the aura of continuity, despite the apparent flux of mortality, can be achieved is by attaining a pervasive sense of tranquillity which reinforces the expansiveness of space. For example, when speaking of the Vale in Book 2, the persona describes the utter solitude of the Vale in the early morning, a solitude which implies the expansiveness of nature and of the self through the aura of calm it nurtures.

Book 3 emphasizes the capacity of the persona, inspired by the diastolic spatiality of nature, to achieve an expansiveness of self. In implying the power of his own imagination the persona reveals the open-ended spatiality of the eye which may shift its attention from the earth to the ocean to the heavens, yet ultimately "could find no surface where its power might sleep" (3.166). Such is the imaginative eye which will develop itself by Book 14 into the majestic mind which transforms an expansive spatiality into a diastolic temporality.

Wordsworth suggests in Book 3 that he is less interested in an expansive spatiality of endless solitude than in an expansive spatiality characterized by human endeavor. Such a philosophy of space is in keeping with Wordsworth's argument in the Preface to *Lyrical Ballads* that the poet should be ultimately concerned with the world of human thoughts, actions, and feelings. In speaking of his experience of the human sphere the persona uses the metaphor of the museum. This is interesting not only because it suggests the closed sense of space of the human world in contrast to the open sense of space of nature, but also because it underscores the element of change which seems to pervade this existence. The profound tranquillity and holy calm of nature is not present, at least at this point of the persona's perceptual and conceptual development, in the world of human endeavor.

At the beginning of Book 4 Wordsworth's persona has a vision of expansive space as he stands alone overlooking "the bed of Windermere" (4.5). In this context the sun has a positive aura because it affirms the openness of the watery space through the expansiveness of its light. This epiphanic moment, signified by the revelation of these forms "with instantaneous burst" (4.10), represents one of the most vital conceptions of space in the early chapters of *The Prelude* because it is generated by a vision of "A universe of Nature's fairest forms" (4.9). The beauty of this seemingly unlimited display of nature's aspects is made more visible and perhaps even more beautiful through the light of the sun.

Occasionally, Wordsworth's persona will imply or proclaim the di-astolic nature of time or his conception of the diastolic capacity of time. In Book 4, for example, in talking about the happiness he en-joyed in making "the circuit of our little lake" (4.138), the persona asserts that "That day consummate happiness was mine / Wide-spread-ing, steady, calm, contemplative" (4.140–41). Whether the four adjec-tives characterize the day or the happiness which the persona feels on this day, they are primarily, at least in their use so far in the poem, aspects of space, of the expansiveness of space.

This is one of the first moments in the poem when the persona adopts the language of space to present the image of time and where the persona foreshadows his ultimate assertion in Book 14 of the diastolic nature of space and time. It is noteworthy here that the pre-sentation of space once again precedes the discussion of time.

Several stanzas later in Book 4 the persona affirms the revitalizing power of solitude to counteract the anguish of everyday mortality. This sense of solitude is described as being "Most potent when im-pressed upon the mind / With an appropriate human centre" (4.358–59). What unites, in the mind of the persona, the three exemplars he offers of this sense of solitude—hermit, votary, and watchman—is their similar experience of an expansive sense of space. Solitude, at this point of *The Prelude* and throughout most of the rest of the work as well, is defined through the qualities of a spatial expansiveness and a profound tranquillity.

The wilderness and the unknown in which these characters partici-pate in their solitude is not inherently tempestuous or violent. Rather, the solitude of the wilderness and the unknown is gracious and be-nign, perhaps because of the innately serene character of these indi-viduals. There is something here of the strategy of "half-creating, half-perceiving" from "Tintern Abbey"—it is through the imagination of the persona, and through the corresponding vision of the characters he envisions in a solitary existential condition, that the solitude may assume "A character of quiet more profound / Than pathless wastes" (4.368–69).

In the next passage of Book 4 there is an episode which prefigures, at least partially, the mountain vision in Book 14. The persona speaks of experiencing a long ascent, the powerful presence of the moon, the stream of water, and a sense of tranquillity—all of these features will be regenerated in the Mt. Snowdon vision in Book 14. Perhaps one might argue that the presence of the tall man in Book 4 is comparable to the rift in the waters in Book 14 which disturbs the quietude of the scene. Yet the man, unlike the rift, ultimately blends into the silence of the surrounding nature.

In Book 5 the expansiveness of space is revealed even in dream. The persona, seated in a sea-side cave reading the adventures of Don Quixote, dreams of "a boundless plain / Of sandy wilderness" (5.71–72). The desolation of this solitude is made more frightening by the appearance, as in the previously mentioned episode in Book 4, of a stranger. This "uncouth shape" (5.75) gives the persona a shell which reveals to him the harmony and dissolution of humankind. Listening to the shell provides the same kind of visionary sense of the future as does the experience of the majestic intellect in Book 14 which can look to the end of time. The crucial difference between the two visions is that the one in Book 5 depicting a destructive end of temporality is motivated by an external source, whereas the one in Book 14 signifying the capacity of the creatively vital mind to envision a positive end of temporality is generated from within.

The two books of which the Arab speaks are of special interest for this discussion of time and space in *The Prelude*. The first book is undisturbed by space or time; the second has a multiplicity of voices and existential forms. Both of these are qualities which will reappear in Book 14 with a dynamic intensity in the individual of majestic mind. The capacity to hold acquaintance with the stars will become the mind which feeds upon infinity and which converses with the spiritual world. The dimension of wedding soul to soul in purest bond of reason will become the powerfully creative mind that can send from itself kindred mutations and that can aspire to create an ecumenical vision from its magnanimous spirit.

At the end of his encounter with the Arab rider the persona sees "a bed of glittering light" (5.129) over half the wilderness. That his companion explains this as "the waters of the deep / Gathering upon us" (5.130–31) prefigures the "roar of waters" (14.59). The destructive imminence of the deluge is only assuaged when the persona suddenly awakes to find himself back in his room.

Bloom argues that "the soul in solitude moves outward by encountering other solitaries" (10). As Wordsworth writes in Book 4, solitude is most powerful when impressed upon the mind with an appropriate human center. This sense of the importance of human reciprocity, as Bloom calls it, intensifies in Book 5 when Wordsworth encounters the Arab who tells him that the stone he carries is "Euclid's Elements"

(5.88) and that the shell is "something of more worth" (5.89), that is, poetry.

Wordsworth's persona finds certain similarities between his own existence and the life of the Arab. Not only does he have the aura of a Don Quixote, but he is "crazed / By love and feeling, and internal thought / Protracted among endless solitudes" (5.145-47). Bloom suggests that such "is a fate that Wordsworth feared for himself, had his sensibility taken too strong control of his reason" (11).

Bloom proceeds to claim that "the Arab's mission, though the poet calls it mad, is very like Wordsworth's own in *The Prelude*. Both desire to save Imagination from the abyss of desert and ocean" (11). Whereas the quest of the Arab appears hopeless before the imminent deluge, "Wordsworth hopes that his own quest will bring the healing waters down, as he pursues his slow, flowing course toward his present freedom" (11).

In Book 6 Wordsworth speaks of his intellectual contemplations at Cambridge leading him to realize the presence of the "one / Supreme Existence" (6.133-34) which is beyond the exigencies of space and time and the vicissitudes of mortality. Such meditation on the existence of "God" (6.139) gives the persona a sense of "transcendent peace" (6.139) which prefigures the serene wisdom of the majestic intellect of Book 14.

After leaving Cambridge for his continental adventure, Wordsworth describes his experience of nature as vitally dynamic. He moves forward on the streams of the Saone and the Rhone with majestic ease. By participating in the fluidity of nature the persona enhances his sense of the expansiveness of space—indeed, his carefree movement on the stream enables him to experience the surrounding natural environment as a "succession without end / Of deep and stately vales" (6.383-84). Spatial expansiveness is linked here with spatial infinitude.

The powerful sense of solitude which the persona has previously achieved and proclaimed the importance of is heightened in his alpine adventure in the ambience of the Convent of Chartreuse. As Wordsworth's persona approaches the Convent of Chartreuse he hears the voice of Nature, which reverberates in from the past to the present, asserting that this special space should be devoted to eternity, indeed, that it should be considered unique in its devotion to eternity. This is a place of primarily expansive spatiality and diastolic temporality which represents a significant precursor to the later vision on Mt. Snowdon.

In its spatiality, exemplified by the idea that entering this domain "leaves far behind life's treacherous vanities" (6.453), the monastery at Chartreuse reveals an aura similar to that of the Grande Chartreuse in Arnold's poem "Stanzas from the Grande Chartreuse" and of Shangri-La in Hilton's *Lost Horizon*. Arnold's and Hilton's spatially hermetic spaces are devoted to eternity as well, though Arnold's is more emotively oriented and Hilton's more aesthetic and cultural.

As the vision on Mt. Snowdon of the majestic intellect is a threshold experience generated by the tension between the roar of waters and the starry heavens and reinforced by the existence of the mind that feeds upon infinity at the edge of the abyss, so the aura, the vitality, of the Chartreuse monastery is defined by its distinctively threshold nature. At the interface of earth and heaven, the monastery is also contiguous with "the sister streams of Life and Death" (6.439). That both streams are described as murmuring gives the entire scene a dynamism and an expansiveness which transforms the hermetic tone to one of orphic, outward-directed energy.

As Shangri-La in *Lost Horizon*, this environment is one pervaded by the "great spirit of human knowledge" (6.450). The crucial difference between the two is that the temporal emphasis in Shangri-La is on the present and the future in contrast to the spirit of knowledge at this point of *The Prelude* being vitalized by the past and the future. Yet, both spaces preserve the capacity to suspend the flux of mortality or to transcend, if only temporarily, mortality.

After leaving the Convent of Chartreuse, Wordsworth's persona proceeds to describe various noteworthy and salient spaces, including the summit of Mont Blanc and the Vale of Chamouny stretching far below. The expansiveness of this vale, now impressive less by its absolute fluidity than by its crystalline, motionless capacity, leads the persona to contemplate the everyday vitality of multiple dimensions of nature. The expansiveness of space generates not only an expansiveness of soul, but also a sense of the diversity and multiplicity of nature.

After crossing the Alps Wordsworth reflects on the power of the imagination which inspires the poetic persona to realize the vital importance of the statement: "Our destiny, our being's heart and home, / Is with infinitude, and only there" (6.604–05). It is through an inward-turning gesture of epiphanic vitality, "when the light of sense / Goes out" (6.600–01), that Wordsworth's persona senses his participation in the diastolic vitality of time. This sense of temporal infinitude links to a belief in eternal hope, effort, expectation, and desire.

This passage apotheosizes the creative mind which is powerful in itself and which does not need external praise. Such a mind that is
"blest in thoughts / That are their own perfection and reward" (6.611–
12) is the precursor of the majestic intellect of Book 14.

In suggesting several lines later that the various aspects of nature in
this mountain landscape, whether the "giddy prospect of the raving
stream" (6.633), the "unfettered clouds" (6.634), or the "Tumult and
peace, the darkness and the light" (6.635), were "all like workings of
one mind" (6.636) the persona again anticipates or foreshadows the
ultimate vision in *The Prelude* of the mind that is "sustained / By
recognitions of transcendent power" (14.74–75) and that may converse with past, present, and future generations of humankind "till
Time shall be no more" (14.111). The essential difference between
the mind of Book 6 and the majestic intellect of Book 14 is that the
latter is more consciously aware of his visionary capacity to communicate with the spiritual world and with multiple generations of humankind until the end of mortality. The self-confidence of the majestic
intellect of Book 14 enables him to develop kindred mutations with a
greater sense of serenity.

The capacity of signifying in one individual, of encompassing in
one creative mind, diverse aspects of nature (a capacity shared by the
mind of Book 6 and the majestic intellect of Book 14) is similar to the
capability of the magnanimous protagonist in Hermann Hesse's
Siddhartha to encompass in himself multiple dimensions of earthly
existence beyond the constraints of space and time:

> He no longer saw the face of his friend Siddhartha. Instead he saw other
> faces, many faces, a long series, a continuous stream of faces—hundreds,
> thousands, which all came and disappeared and yet all seemed to be there at
> the same time, which all continually changed and renewed themselves and
> which were yet all Siddhartha. (121)

Siddhartha, in his capacity to embrace all these forms and establish a
continuity of kindred mutations, embodies the vitality of the creatively
dynamic intellect of Wordsworth's persona as "a mind sustained / By
recognitions of transcendent power / In sense conducting to ideal
form" (14.74–76).

The mind of Book 6 of *The Prelude* assumes in itself "Characters
of the great Apocalypse" (6.638) which are the "types and symbols of
Eternity" (6.639) and shows the ability to fuse these complementary
yet opposite experiences of "Apocalypse" and "Eternity" in a threshold realm of creative vitality. It is at this threshold moment, or thresh-

old succession of moments, at the interface of the raving stream and the unfettered clouds, tumult and peace, darkness and light, apocalypse and eternity that the persona glimpses the diastolic, expansive nature of space and time. The cyclicality implied by line 640 in Book 6 ("Of first, and last, and midst, and without end") will be transformed to the cessation of Time in Book 14. The vision of the ultimate atemporality of Time reveals the extraordinary power of the majestic intellect which is only intuited in Book 6.

The capacity of Wordsworth's persona to encompass in himself diverse features of nature is reinforced by his desire to preserve and strengthen a continuity of self and nature. The persona who says of the lake near the end of Book 6 that its beauty remains with him especially because he feels intimately connected to it believes in the importance of a continuity of self and nature. In conceiving of himself as a spiritual and physical dimension of the lake's domain in saying "Like a breeze / Or sunbeam over your domain I passed" (6.675–76), the persona affirms a sense of continuity with nature as powerful as it is serene.

In the passage starting with line 592 the persona suggests the inadequacy of language to capture the power of the imagination. Yet, in the same breath he asserts the dynamic vitality of the imagination. The imagination of the creatively vital individual has the potential to experience epiphanic moments such as the revelation of the world of nature or spirit beyond everyday mortality. At this moment the persona realizes that his destiny, the destiny of those individuals infused with the power of the imagination, "is with infinitude and only there" (6.605).

In Book 7 Wordsworth not only stresses the continuity of the self with nature, but also reaffirms the importance of the threshold experience. After the hour of sunset one evening, at the threshold of light and darkness (both indoors and outside) Wordsworth's persona hears "a choir of redbreasts" (7.21). He is inspired to go outside and observes "a glow-worm underneath a dusky plume / Or canopy of yet unwithered fern" (7.33–34). In this twilight ambience Wordsworth experiences pristine qualities of sound and silence. The pristine aura of this moment enables him later to experience the threshold ambience of the majestic intellect as a timeless continuum of past, present, and future generations.

In Book 8 Wordsworth affirms the importance of Nature as his aesthetic guide and inspiration. Geoffrey Hartman writes in "The Romance of Nature and the Negative Way" that nature for Wordsworth "is not an 'object' but a presence and a power; a motion and a spirit; not something to be worshiped and consumed, but always a guide leading beyond itself" (60). In saying that his heart was first opened to the sense of natural beauty in the "domains of rural peace" (8.73), Wordsworth is once again not only privileging the dimension of space but also critiquing the incapacity of the urban environment and its turbulence to arouse the same aesthetic vitality in him. He speaks of his home environment as a "tract more exquisitely fair / Than that famed paradise of ten thousand trees" (8.75–76). As beautiful as this "sumptuous dream of flowery lawns, with domes / Of pleasure sprinkled over" (8.84–85) is, the paradise of his home is far more beautiful.

Such a vital devotion to the landscape of youth is found with similar intensity in the affection of John Constable for his childhood landscape. Indeed, Constable's creation of the aesthetic, spiritual aura of the Stour River valley is comparable to Wordsworth's creation of the aesthetic, spiritual aura of the Lake District. Wordsworth's recollection, as Constable's, of the paradise landscape of youth is not merely praise of nature—it is also a praise of the individual laborer, of the man working for himself in a state of relative independence.

This section of The Prelude culminates in Wordsworth's praise of the shepherd who, in representing the noblest qualities of the human spirit, becomes an integral part of nature. In the midst of this praise of the shepherd Wordsworth lauds as well the openness, the expansiveness of space to inspire the shepherd. In presenting various aspects of nature such as moors, mountains, and vales, Wordsworth implies the capacity of the openness of space to reinforce the sense of freedom of the shepherd. As earlier in The Prelude, so in this context the openness of space is used to challenge or counteract the seemingly inevitable flux of time. For example, to elude the "lingering dews of morn / Smoke around him" (8.244–45) the shepherd wanders from hill to hill. Through the medium of space the shepherd seeks not only an escape from the exigencies of mortality, but also a transformation of time.

Perhaps because he is beset by various dangers of the solitudes through which he wanders as "a freeman, wedded to his life of hope / And hazard" (8.253–54), the shepherd is granted a nobility of stature by Wordsworth's critical eye. Not only does the presence of the shepherd exert a dynamic emotional-spiritual influence over his immediate natural environment, but he appears as a giant in the mist with "his sheep like Greenland bears" (8.267). The power of the shepherd's presence is amplified or intensified by the surrounding nature. For example, as he steps "beyond the boundary line of some hill-shadow" (8.268) the form of the shepherd is illuminated by the setting sun.

Such a moment of radiance seems to be an aspect of the sense sublime "Whose dwelling is the light of setting suns" (97) that Wordsworth describes in "Tintern Abbey." In concluding this section by depicting another appearance of the shepherd as "a solitary object and sublime" (8.272), Wordsworth presents him as a figure with the stature of the persona in C. D. Friedrich's *Traveller Looking Over a Sea of Fog* (1815). The similarity of these conceptions is reinforced by the shared conviction of Wordsworth and Friedrich in the capacity of such creatively vital individuals to signify the "sanctity of Nature given to man" (8.295).

The portrayal of the shepherd in this section is also important because it reveals qualities which will later be emphasized as essential for the majestic intellect of Book 14. The shepherd is by his creatively vital nature the precursor and harbinger of the majestic intellect not only with respect to his magnanimous soul and his capacity to "send abroad / Kindred mutations" (14.93–94) into his immediate natural environment, but also in light of the sense of freedom he represents. The nobility of the shepherd as of the majestic intellect of Book 14 ultimately leads Wordsworth to reaffirm his "faith in life endless, the sustaining thought / Of human Being, Eternity, and God" (14.204–05).

The potential of a special natural space to exert a consistently affirmative influence on the persona is proclaimed in Book 8 in the depiction of the grove "whose boughs / Stretch from the western marge of Thurston-mere" (8.458–59). As in previous passages in *The Prelude* it is the golden light of the setting sun which inspires the emotional and spiritual energy of the moment. As the golden light of the setting sun rests in silent beauty on the ridge of a high hill, the persona declares that wherever the future will take him he will always think back on the beauty of this natural domain to encourage and inspire him.

This devotion to special natural places which will guide the persona congenially through the flux of mortality is expressed with similar conviction and intensity in the poetry of the nineteenth-century German Romantic Joseph von Eichendorff. For example, in his poem "Abschied" ("Farewell") the persona, in departing from a beautiful natural space of the kind of personal importance that Wordsworth and Constable ascribe to their childhood places, asserts that his heart will never grow old in his wanderings through the world of mortality as long as he may reflect upon the emotional, spiritual, and aesthetic beauty of his beloved forest.

Wordsworth distinguishes between at least two complementary, if not essentially antithetical, dimensions of time. In contrast to mortality, to the evanescence of animate life, thought, action, there is Time, which is a sense of mortality raised to a higher power, to a condition of apparent atemporality. In Book 8 when Wordsworth speaks of memory as divinity he describes the latter dimension of time: "All that took place within me came and went / As in a moment; yet with Time it dwells / And grateful memory, as a thing divine" (8.557–59). This sense of Time is both mortal and atemporal; in signifying memory as a divine condition it seems to anticipate the sense of timelessness in Book 14, but it is still more linked to evanescence than to permanence. The third dimension of time is seen in Book 14 when the persona anticipates an existential condition when "Time shall be no more" (14.111). This sense of time is a timeless, atemporal time beyond the temporal mortality and the atemporal mortality of Book 8.

Herbert Lindenberger writes in "The Structural Unit: 'Spots of Time'" that the personal past, "the quest for which is the substance of *The Prelude*, is not recreated in and for itself, but only within the perspective of the present, through which alone it derives meaning" (77–78). It is the timeless, or atemporal, present which encompasses the past in an existential condition of epiphanic vitality, as the majestic intellect of Book 14 embraces in himself kindred manifestations of nature.

From Book 9 to Book 11 of *The Prelude* Wordsworth speaks of his experiences in France, especially during the time of the French Revolution. One of his first critiques of the excesses of the revolution is that an atmosphere of terrible agitation and strife was produced. Wordsworth describes in Book 9 this unquiet commotion as a mockery "Of history, the past and that to come" (9.169). In light of this statement, which is presented in temporal terms, perhaps one could argue that Wordsworth is so interested in space because he views it as a means of ameliorating or transforming the anguish of mortality. Yet, the kind of space that he ultimately needs is not the flatland, which he describes in this passage as "the land all swarmed with passion, like a plain / Devoured by locusts" (9.175–76), but a place that affords a certain physical distance from and a novel emotional and intellectual perspective on the context of the unquiet commotion.

Raymond Williams speaks in *Culture and Society: 1780–1950* of the vital influence which the French Revolution had on its contemporary political and social context, suggesting that the hope, energy, and vision accompanying the French Revolution was not merely background material but "the mould in which general experience was cast" (30–31). This sense of the positive influence of the French Revolution is shared by Wordsworth's contemporary, William Hazlitt, who asserted in *The Spirit of the Age* that the innovations in Wordsworth's poetry derived from the spirit of the sentiments and opinions that produced the French Revolution. J. S. Mill shared Hazlitt's conviction, stressing in his essays on *The Spirit of the Age* the animating, revolutionary spirit of the age which was inspiring and stimulating a more vital literary expression.

The negative influence of the French Revolution on Wordsworth, an influence which lasted through the rest of his life, is already seen in 1792 in his awareness of the horrific violence which permeated the revolutionary ambience. As late as 1840 Wordsworth told Thomas Carlyle that he had witnessed the execution on October 7, 1793, of the journalist Gorsas, an event especially disturbing because it raised the question "Where will it end, when you have set an example in this kind" (Hanley 47)?

Wordsworth's quest for the magic mountain is a quest for a profoundly tranquil space beyond the atmosphere of terror and violence of such events as the French Revolution and beyond the social unrest in England, while at the same time preserving the humanitarian dimension of the revolutionary spirit. Wordsworth's persona on Mt. Snowdon aspires to achieve the "revolution of consciousness in mankind" in the spirit of Friedrich Schelling's assertion of the purpose of his philosophy "to point out to the human spirit a new road, to give bruised and battered spirits courage and inner strength" (Abrams 26).

In portraying the unique officer whom he meets in France, Wordsworth presents an individual who is at least to some extent a precursor of the majestic intellect of Book 14. This individual is depicted as a man of noble spirit, generous heart, humane soul, and wise intellect. His death, fighting for liberty and against deluded humankind is a great loss for Wordsworth. Yet, the memory of his nobility of soul is preserved in the creative persona of Book 14. Wordsworth shared his friend's idealistic conviction that a better, more humane world would emerge in the near future.

In the essay "The Revolutionary 'I': Wordsworth and the Politics of Self-Presentation" A. Nichols argues that the Wordsworthian first person develops out of the interaction of "complementary and conflicting discourses: the rhetoric of the French Revolution, eighteenth-century ideas about the profession of authorship, and Wordsworth's need to create an identity whose apparent center is at once poetical and philosophical" (66). In suggesting that what is revolutionary in the lyrical sources and lyrics of *The Prelude* is "their evolution of a new version of the autobiographical 'I'" (66), Nichols claims that in Goslar, where Wordsworth produced the lyrical fragments that eventually became the source texts for *The Prelude*, he "does not start telling the story of his past life so much as he begins writing a version of his life that can become his story" (67).

Nichols says that "by the time he returned from Goslar, Wordsworth had begun to connect his poetics as social practice with a specific view of his profession as a calling" (76). Nichols proceeds to suggest that, in the spirit of Wordsworth's statement in the Preface to *The Excursion* of how its author had returned to his native mountains, "retirement became Wordsworth's means of beginning a career" (76). In creating an identity whose center is simultaneously poetical and philosophical Wordsworth's persona prepares himself to achieve ultimately the stature of the majestic intellect who can encompass various dimensions of the world in the holistically unified aura of the creative self.

In Book 10 Wordsworth gradually regains his faith in humanity and in justice as some of the perpetrators of the excesses of the French Revolution lose their authority. At the beginning of Book 11 Wordsworth is confident that a sense of renovation will proceed for "Authority in France / Put on a milder face" (11.1–2) and "Terror had ceased" (11.2). The glorious renovation will be more vital if it learns from and derives its power and wisdom at least to some extent from the "One great society alone on earth: / The noble Living and noble Dead" (11.393–94). For these are the majestic intellects of the world, the souls of magnanimous spirit and of more than mortal privilege.

In Book 12 of *The Prelude* Wordsworth affirms that nature may comfort and encourage him vitally when the world of everyday mortality becomes oppressive or painful. As in John Constable's *The Hay Wain* (1821) or C.D. Friedrich's *The Solitary Tree* (1822) it is a vital sense of natural space (the sense of space the protagonist gains through a sensitive appreciation of nature) that gives the persona emotional inspiration and aesthetic-spiritual stimulation.

In roaming "from hill to hill, from rock to rock" (12.143) in search of new forms, Wordsworth's persona is also questing for a "wider

empire for the sight" (12.145). One is reminded of Jane Eyre's belief
in the importance of the horizon in developing her visionary imagination. As this passage progresses Wordsworth describes "a maid / A
young enthusiast" (12.151–52) who was attuned "by her benign simplicity" (12.161) and by her "perfect happiness of soul" (12.162) to
every scene that presented itself to her view. Similarly, the personae
in Constable's *Hay Wain* and Friedrich's *The Solitary Tree* savor the
relatively enclosed and hermetic space in which they exist.
Wordsworth's persona, though appreciating the beauty of hermetic
spaces, implies that he is not content with this strategy. His creativity
derives to a considerable extent from a complementary awareness both
of the beauty of hermetic spaces and the grandeur and sublimity of
diastolic space.

As in the Immortality Ode Wordsworth speaks in *The Prelude* of
the significance of "spots of time" (12.208) that may nourish and
invisibly repair our minds beset by the cares of everyday mortality and
locates the source of the "spots of time" in childhood. Bloom asserts
that "the function of the spots of time is to enshrine the spirit of the
past for future restoration" (21). The "spots of time" are moments of
heightened emotional, intellectual, or spiritual awareness similar in
intensity to Pater's moments of "quickened, multiplied consciousness."
Whereas for Pater in *The Renaissance* to achieve the most intense
impression possible was the great objective of living and to seize and
transfix this moment became an aesthetic duty, for Wordsworth in
The Prelude the recovery of the past might enable the poet, the artist, who is most able to appreciate these "spots of time," to achieve a
faith in the integrity of the self to prepare him for the future.

One such epiphanic moment which Wordsworth describes is an
experience on the eve of the Christmas holiday when he, in an an-
guished state of mind, went forth into the fields. In anticipation of
foreshadowing of his adventure of Mt. Snowdon in Book 14,
Wordsworth speaks of his ascending a crag and experiencing a misty,
wild atmosphere. In this threshold experience the persona on the crag
is sheltered or trapped between images of light and darkness (it is day,
yet it is a tempestuous, dark day) and life and death (on his right hand
a single sheep, on his left hand a blasted hawthorn).

Moreover, the image of being shrouded by mist which only occasionally diminishes or evaporates to provide glimpses "of the copse /
And plain beneath" (12.304–05) suggests a threshold experience of
emotional and spiritual intensity—this is affirmed in the death of his
father soon after. This threshold epiphany becomes meaningful for

Wordsworth when he observes the seemingly antithetical features as complementary dimensions of an existential whole. He speaks of the diverse elements, the wind and rain, the sheep and the hawthorn, as "kindred spectacles and sounds" (12.324). By assimilating the conflicting aspects of this moment into a harmonious whole, by viewing them as a unified vision, Wordsworth is able to overcome the existential fragility and despair which might otherwise ensue. Wordsworth suggests further that his creativity is most stimulated at such a threshold moment.

David Simpson in "The Spots of Time: Spaces for Refiguring" claims that the spots of time, especially the poet coming upon the gibbet in early childhood and the poet climbing to the top of a crag to try to observe the horses which are to carry him home, "seem to involve a recognition and acceptance of the notion that the figurings of the moment are always displaced, often painfully, into subsequent and ongoing refigurings" (142). Simpson proceeds to describe these refigurings as forms that "are not prefigured by others, and are integrally educative rather than merely habit-forming" (142). In its emphasis on a continuous growth process this capacity for refigurings affirms the persona's potential for participating in and shaping an expansive sense of time.

In Book 13 Wordsworth's persona prepares himself increasingly more for his ultimate vision in the final book. He proclaims nature to be the source not only of his creative power, the "energy by which he seeks the truth" (13.8), but also of the profound tranquillity which pervades the genial spirit. In enlarging the horizon of his mind, the persona asserts that he devoted himself to the intellectual eye in his quest for great truths. Although the persona admits that other environments may be a source for such truths, he concludes by declaring that there is no ambience as inspirational and enriching as that of Nature.

The image of the path leading towards the horizon signifies one of Wordsworth's perpetual spots of time. As familiar as the "windings of a public way" (13.143) may be, they have exerted and still exert a powerful stimulus on the persona's imagination. The sense of expansive windings, representing "an invitation into space / Boundless, or guide into eternity" (13.149-50), affirms the diastolic spatiality which energizes the persona.

Wordsworth continues this argument by claiming that the "wanderers of the earth" (13.154) have always possessed a certain emotional-spiritual grandeur in his mind. Wordsworth concludes this passage by implying that those individuals who have a diastolic sense of space (and who believe in the importance of an expansive space) are able to see into the depths of human souls. Through his diastolic experience of space the persona heightens and enriches his burgeoning understanding of the universal heart, of the human condition. Gill stresses the importance of the complementarity of imagination and love for the creative self to achieve such an understanding of the human condition: "Imagination is presented as the power that enables Man to convert into knowledge that which he perceives, to shape his world. In alliance with Love it binds him to his fellow beings" (239).

An interesting passage about the complementarity of space and time occurs when the persona asserts that his youthful spirit was raised when he was once among the wilds of Sarum's Plain. As the persona wanders across the pastoral dawns, as he experiences an expansive spatiality and an increasing solitude, he also attains an expanding sense of time, a vision of the past as "Time with his retinue of ages fled / Backwards" (13.318–19). In observing the ancient past of England, an ambience of the living and the dead, the persona anticipates the capacity of the majestic intellect in the final book to communicate with past generations of humankind.

As this vision of the past continues, Wordsworth's persona sees the stone work of the Druids, representing their knowledge of the heavens, and observes the "long-bearded teachers, with white wands / Uplifted" (13.345–46) pointing towards the starry sky and the plain in a melodious moment of universal harmony. Not only does the persona envision the past in this threshold experience as dynamic as the previous threshold moments at the interface of light and darkness, the living and the dead, but he participates in its vitality. The persona in this passage strengthens his visionary imagination as well by aspiring to achieve a creative and enduring work which may become "A power like one of Nature's" (13.312).

In Book 13 Wordsworth's persona asserts the importance of emotional vitality, especially an emotional vitality connected with wisdom, by stressing the significance of the "feeling intellect." It is this "feeling intellect" which can express a genuinely fraternal love in a spirit of humanitarian vitality. In distinguishing his approach from the approach of the historians who are interested in describing "power and energy detached / From moral purpose" (13.43–44), Wordsworth's persona asserts the significance of looking upon the world and especially upon the "unassuming things that hold / A silent station in this beauteous world" (13.46–47) with a sense of appreciative love. As the circumference of his imagination is enlarged by thoughts of ever new delight, the persona becomes more desirous of participating in the "energy by which he seeks the truth" (13.8) and which derives from the vitality of nature.

In Book 14 Wordsworth's persona experiences the epiphanic vision on Mt. Snowdon. The stream of moonlight combined with "the roar of waters" (14.59) creates a moment of extraordinary sensory vitality. This experience of the power of nature suggests to Wordsworth's persona the presence of a "majestic intellect" (14.67), of a "mind / That feeds upon infinity" (14.70–71). This majestic intellect is capable of experiencing both "kairos" and "Aion" and of transforming "kairos" to "Aion."

Panofsky says that in classical art Time was described either as fleeting Opportunity ("kairos") or creative Eternity ("Aion"). In the moment of fleeting opportunity the individual "feels himself to be actively and totally fitted to the world about him" (Beer 32). In the experience of "Aion" there is an influx of visionary power—the individual "is so possessed by inward imagination as to feel no transience in the passing of time" (Beer 32). The "spots of time" of Wordsworth's persona in The Prelude may signify either an experience of "kairos" or "Aion," yet ultimately he transforms "kairos" to "Aion," for the majestic intellect represents an influx and diffusion of visionary power.

The diastolic spatiality of "Tintern Abbey" and the Immortality Ode becomes the timeless space of Book 14 of The Prelude. This timeless space is both an expansive landscape of the mind and a dynamic landscape of nature. There is throughout The Prelude and in the last book in particular a correlation or reflection of mind and nature which enhances the power of both. In suggesting that the higher minds of the universe "can send abroad / Kindred mutations" (14.93–94) from their own vital selves, Wordsworth creates an existential aura which reaffirms the reflection of humankind and nature.

The "faith that looks through death" (185) and the philosophic mind of the Immortality Ode become the powerful creative intellect of Book 14 of The Prelude. One of the most vital characteristics of this majestic intellect is its capacity "to hold fit converse with the spiritual world" (14.108) and with past, present, and future generations of humankind until time shall no longer exist. The realization of this capability is a dynamic sign of the success of the magic mountain adventure for this persona.

We have seen that the sense of space generates the sense of time in Wordsworth. In "Tintern Abbey" there is a diastolic sense of space and a sense of time that is both hermetic and orphic, hermetic in the sense that the persona is aware of mortality, orphic in the sense that the persona believes intuitively that an expansiveness of space may lead to a sense of expanding time. In "Nuns Fret Not" there is a hermetic sense of space that is really innately diastolic and expansive. The Immortality Ode offers a diastolic awareness of space that encompasses multiple dimensions of the natural environment and a sense of time founded on "the faith that looks through death" (185). The power of this diastolic sense of space and time is energized by the epiphanic vitality of "those first affections" (148) which "are yet the fountain-light of all our day" (151). The diastolic sense of space is affirmed in the image of the "immortal sea" (163), the vision of which will perpetually revitalize the persona.

One may describe the epiphanic vitality of those "first affections" (148) and "shadowy recollections" (149) as moments in the dynamic present of things past. In contrast to Book 14 of *The Prelude* which motivates its expansive sense of space and time by an emphasis on the present of things present complemented by the present of things past and future, the Immortality Ode stresses the supremely influential role of significant past moments to inspire and sustain the persona.

The motion and the spirit that move through all things which the persona senses in "Tintern Abbey" are comparable to the image of the "Kindred mutations" (14.94) in *The Prelude*. The difference between the two contexts is that in "Tintern Abbey" the persona senses the motion and the spirit that permeates all things but is not necessarily the agent of that motion. On the other hand, in Book 14 of *The Prelude* the majestic intellect which is revealed to the persona and which is a manifestation of the persona's own mind, acts as the generating spirit which "can send abroad / Kindred mutations" (14.93–94) and may actively shape the spirit that moves through all things.

As in the previous poems, so in *The Prelude* a sense of space generates or leads to a sense of time. The persona in Book 14 has a vision of the light of the moon spreading over the "billowy ocean" (14.55) and of the "roar of waters" (14.59) emerging from the rift before he expresses a sense of time. The persona experiences the expansiveness of light and space before he envisions the mind "that feeds upon infinity" (14.71).

Alan Liu describes the expansiveness of the self in *The Prelude* as "Wordsworth's moment of Absolute Knowledge" (447) which involves "the knowledge of many things" (447). Liu proceeds to argue that "Snowdon is a vision of poetic Imagination that has 'usurped' upon the world in which actual usurpers rise to power" (447).

The capacity of the majestic intellect to create and to participate in an expansiveness of self, space, and time is affirmed in the lines that stress the significance of the "mind sustained / By recognitions of transcendent power" (14.74–75). In the following line, "In sense conducting to ideal form," the persona implies the potential of the majestic intellect to be an active part of an ambience of spatial expansiveness, an ambience aspiring to encompass ideal forms. Line 77, "In soul of more than mortal privilege," suggests the capacity of the majestic intellect to challenge and transcend mortality. These few lines are important not only because they delineate qualities of the majestic intellect, but also because, in representing a thematic unity, they affirm the interrelation of space and time.

In Book 14 the persona suggests that the individual who has achieved a diastolic sense of space and time, who has participated in an aura of the expansiveness of space and time, has attained a condition of genuine liberty. An essential, perhaps the essential, dimension of this sense of liberty is the development of the imagination which Wordsworth characterizes in Book 14 as "but another name for absolute power / And clearest insight, amplitude of mind, / And reason in her most exalted mood" (14.190–92). The phrase "amplitude of mind" (14.191) especially reaffirms the importance of a diastolically vital imagination, the development and strengthening of which leads to "Faith in life endless, the sustaining thought / Of human Being, Eternity and God" (14.204–05).

In aspiring to achieve and preserve a diastolic sense of space and time the individual of majestic intellect develops a "Faith in life endless," a faith which unifies the strivings of humanity, time and the divine for eternity. Through his experience of this faith on the mountain the creatively vital persona shapes the diastolic sense of space into a simultaneously dynamic awareness of the expansiveness of time.

The Prelude, as Wlecke and others have argued, can be seen as representing the development of a sublime consciousness in the spirit of Longinus' sense of the sublime as signifying an uplifting of the soul and an expansion of the mind and its powers. R. P. Knight in an *Analytical Inquiry into the Principles of Taste* emphasizes this essential feature of the theory of the sublime of Longinus: "Longinus observes that the effect of the sublime is to lift up the soul; to exalt it into ecstasy; so that, participating . . . of the splendors of the divinity it becomes filled with joy and exultation."[1] This sense of "participating of the splendors of the divinity" is crucial not only to Wordsworth's majestic intellect of *The Prelude* but also to the characters in Hilton's *Lost Horizon* who appreciate the sublime serenity of Shangri-La.

Wordsworth's capacity to appreciate the sublime develops in his youth, for he speaks of the vitality which was conferred by early converse with the works of the divine. After emphasizing the pure grandeur of the mind which confronts habitually the majesty of nature, Wlecke asserts that "through constant 'converse' with these hills, through a deepening comprehension of their eternity . . . the mind grows into an awareness . . . of how indeed the 'soul' has a 'prospect' of 'majesty' precisely because the mind is eternal" (61). The sublime consciousness which Wordsworth develops is affirmed in his intuition, expressed in Book 2 of *The Prelude*, for example, of the one life in all things. The expansiveness of self through space and time is reinforced not only in the experience of continuity through natural piety in the spirit of the introductory lines of the Immortality Ode, but also in the sentiment of Being in which the persona of sublime consciousness participates and which permeates and unifies the phenomenal world.

Of Book 14 of *The Prelude* Geoffrey Hartman writes in *The Unremarkable Wordsworth* that "Snowdon is a vision of mastery, though a peculiar one" (103), especially in the sense that "there is no single locus of majesty or mastery" (103). Perhaps there seems to be an absence of a cosmological or ontological position to resolve the tension between the powers of sound and light, nature and mind, because this position exists in the expansive mind of the creative persona who encompasses the disparate elements in his dynamic self.

Hartman argues further that the ascent of Snowdon "presents a sequence of two moments curiously harmonized" (172), the fusion of sight and sound, the light of the moon and the roar of waters. Of this moment Hartman writes: "Spotting the moon fulfills his hope in an unexpected way, which also foreshortens time. The mind of the poet

---

[1] Richard Payne Knight, *Analytical Inquiry into the Principles of Taste* (London, 1805) 329.

is disoriented; but the time is lengthened as the sight of the moon-struck scene takes over in a kind of silent harmonization" (172). Through the aura of silent harmonization such a lengthening of time affirms the spatial and temporal expansiveness of the creative self.

The organic nature of Wordsworth's thought and his subjectivity, in which, Hartman argues, "the starting point for authentic reflection is placed in the individual consciousness" (9), enable and stimulate the consciousness of the creative self to burgeon expansively. Such an organically developing consciousness encompasses not only a process of self-revitalization which signifies the dynamic continuity of the self but also a capacity to appreciate and understand the expansiveness of space and time.

In the spirit of his emphasis on the organically developing nature of the majestic intellect, Hartman asserts that *The Prelude* is "a 'Bildungsroman' that takes the child from solipsism to society and from his unconsciously apocalyptic mind, dreaming of an utterly different world, to a sense of realities" (16). Hartman proceeds to describe *The Prelude* as "the epic of civilization, the epic of the emergence of an individual consciousness out of a field of forces that includes imagination, nature, and society" (16). Yet the consciousness that will ultimately come to a sense of realities is still capable of dreaming of utterly different worlds which may border on, interact with, and encompass eternity, the eternal permanences of nature, as well as infinity.

Chapter 2

Matthew Arnold

In the *Fortnightly Review* Algernon Swinburne praises Matthew Arnold in such statements as: "No one has in like measure that tender and final quality of touch which tempers the excessive light and suffuses the refluent shade. . . . His tones and effects are pure, lucid, aerial" (168–69). Some of the qualities which Swinburne ascribes to the poetry of Arnold are essential as well to the representation of the poet in Arnold's poetry, especially the capacity for clarity and nobility of thought. G. Robert Stange emphasizes the significance of similar qualities in his discussion of "Stanzas in Memory of the Author of 'Obermann'": "For Arnold, Senancour was not a great writer; he was merely the finest example of a certain kind of reclusive writer. The wise poet achieves a different form of austerity; he must come to terms with the world, master it, and yet retain his own inner quiet and integrity of being" (75). These are qualities which are essential to Arnold's creative persona who is comparable to Wordsworth's majestic intellect of *The Prelude*.

Arnold's persona must undergo a "magic mountain" experience before he may truly realize the importance of and become such a "wise poet." Arnold's "magic mountain" experience is a quest for a profoundly serene wisdom beyond the frailties and miseries of commercial, industrial Victorian England. This quest, which develops from "Resignation" through "Stanzas in Memory of the Author of 'Obermann'" and "Empedocles on Etna" to the culminating moment in "Stanzas from the Grande Chartreuse," is initiated and precipitated by the sense of anxiety which Arnold and some of his contemporaries felt about the intellectual and spiritual condition of Victorian society.

Humphry House in his essay "The Mood of Doubt" captures the essence of this sense of anxiety which challenged and undermined the seeming optimism of the Victorian period. He speaks of various events between 1820 and 1870 that made the future seem insecure: "major epidemics of cholera in '32, '48–9, and other lesser outbreaks; chances of revolution in '32, '39, '48; great disturbances in parts of the country in '50, and riots that thoroughly disturbed Matthew Arnold in '66; major scares of foreign invasion in the fifties, from Napoleon III" (72).

House proceeds to argue that the increased tempo of life during this period and the concomitant increase in social and economic problems "caused, both in the lives of individuals and in the political life of the nation, further difficulties and also discomfort, doubt, and hysterical impatience leading almost to despair" (73). Not only Carlyle and Thackeray, but Arnold as well was strongly affected by this permeating Angst. Such a sense of doubt and despair was heightened by the frustration at the inability of the age to solve these problems effectively—the slowness of reform is exemplified by the development of the English Public Health Act, which, when it was first put on the Statute Book, was conspicuously inadequate and had to be gradually modified.

House concludes by saying that the sense of doubt of the early and mid-Victorians was intensified because they were trying to unify, unsuccessfully, incompatible opposites: "they clung to an immortality that should not include the possible justice of Eternal Punishment; they wanted a system of administration which should be efficient without expense; in face of repeated and ferocious strikes and riots they clung to the doctrine that the interests of employers and employed were identical" (76–77). Like some of Arnold's personae, the early and mid-Victorians were caught between two worlds without being essentially at home in either.

One viable approach for the creative self to the experience of despair was the capacity to develop a calm, ecumenical vision of the world in the spirit of Arnold's "Resignation":

> The poet, to whose mighty heart
> Heaven doth a quicker pulse impart,
> Subdues that energy to scan
> Not his own course, but that of man. (144–47)

The serenity of such a vision is achieved in a Stoic detachment from the chaotic vicissitudes of modern life, which may take the form of the flight of the Scholar Gypsy deeper into the wood or the form of the return of the persona of "Stanzas in Memory of the Author of 'Obermann'" to the world of mortality which he evaluates at a critical distance.

In "Resignation" Arnold portrays the poet as a creatively vital individual with a magnanimous, mighty heart who is inspired by heaven to observe the world of humankind. However, he should describe and interpret the feelings, thoughts, and actions of the human sphere not by participating actively in everyday mortality but by maintaining a Stoic detachment from life. The poet is not alone when he is distant from the crowd because he is always an integral part of life and because he is an everpresent dimension of and contributor to the universal soul.

Not only does the poet feel more deeply, but he also has the capability to breathe, when he wishes to, "immortal air / Where Orpheus and Homer are" (207–08). The poet in "Resignation" is not bound to any sphere of activity—he may move freely from one realm of thought and feeling to another, never losing the elasticity and elusiveness of his creative dynamism. This elasticity of movement is differentiated from a similar elasticity in "Empedocles on Etna" by the fact that it is linked with a positive sense of accomplishment. While Empedocles moves from one sphere to another to resolve his inner pain and restlessness, the poet of "Resignation" moves freely between existential domains because he wants to embrace artistically the breadth and depth of human existence.

Lines 231–244 of "Resignation" elaborate Arnold's conception of the poet, the individual who has the potential to develop an expansive sense of space and time. Arnold's poet has an insight and wisdom which pierces the veneer of everyday mortality and sees the essence of things beyond mere appearance. Arnold's poet is worthy of praise not only because of his inspirational creative vitality, because of his wisdom and sensitive understanding of humankind, nature, and the divine, but also because he "treads at ease life's uncheer'd ways" (237) in a spirit of calm detachment.

This strategy of calm detachment is made the more vital if the art motivated by it is dedicated to joy. Roberts argues in *Arnold and God* that "art—which for Arnold is poetry—has a way of transcending time in achieving the needed joy" (82). There is an affirmational undertone to Arnold's depiction of the poet in "Resignation" which is gradually diminished in poems such as "Empedocles on Etna." The theme of resignation in the poem applies literally and symbolically to the poet, who exists at an emotional, intellectual distance from everyday reality, and also to the individual who is inspired, perhaps both by the poet's sagacity as well as by his own growing self-awareness, to realize the vanity of life while trying to shape some meaningfulness from it.

Stange argues that "Resignation" describes a state of mind which is requisite to the creation and enjoyment of poetry: "'resignation' is a spiritual condition, the moral attitude of the wise man and, for the aspiring poet, philosophical preparation for achievement" (54). Stange proceeds to claim in *Matthew Arnold—The Poet as Humanist* that for Arnold (and especially for the Arnold of "Resignation") the deepest insight of the poet "is at once ethical and aesthetic. Poetry is by nature, Arnold would insist, normative, and the finest wisdom provides a rule of life as well as art" (64). Stange suggests that the Stoic resignation which the poet learns from nature is essential to wise conduct and to the development of a peaceful spirit.

Park Honan affirms the necessity for the poet who judges "vain beforehand human cares" of the sense of resignation "which is recommended by Epictetus and especially by the Hindu *Bhagavad Gita*" (178). Honan proceeds to say of Arnold that "if he sees the resignation a creative poet needs, he has not achieved it" (179). In suggesting that Arnold as poet has not yet achieved the inner harmony which the poem emphasizes Honan says that "he is perhaps a neophyte Strayed Reveller rather than a Wise Bard or an Olympian" (179).

In the opening two stanzas of "Resignation" Arnold distinguishes between those individuals in the course of history who felt that they had to be active, even aggressively active, to attain a sense of accomplishment and those individuals who appear to be passive and "whom an unblamed serenity / Hath freed from passions" (23–24). Another essential difference between these types of individuals is that the former are bound to the flux of time and subject to the vicissitudes of space whereas the latter are resigned to their seemingly timeless serenity and do not try to confront aggressively the presence of mortality.

Although aware of the evanescence of mortal life, Arnold seems to imply the capacity of certain special places to confer a sense of timelessness, if only temporary, on the persona who is sensitively aware of his natural environment. From line 40 to line 85 Arnold describes an event which occured ten years prior to the experience of the poem. Space and time are presented realistically as parameters of human experience—there is no explicit interest in transcendence, in challenging the flux of time.

In the next section (lines 86–107) the persona describes his journey with his sister, to whom the poem is addressed, over the same path. The natural environment is depicted as unchanged since their adventure ten years ago—for example, "The self-same shadows now, as then / Play through this grassy upland glen" (98–99). This nature, vital in its own hermetic cyclicality, does not try to expand beyond itself. The persona, as the natural ambience he describes, is also not interested in transcendence, in challenging and transmuting the rush of hours which constitutes mortal existence. Instead, like Conway in Hilton's *Lost Horizon*, he aspires to slow down the pace of time and in such a way create a sense of atemporality.

As Wordsworth's poet in the Preface to *Lyrical Ballads*, so Arnold's poet has a more lively sensibility, a greater knowledge of human nature, and a more comprehensive soul than most of his fellow beings. Although Arnold's poet maintains a Stoic detachment from the world, he is an integral part of the whole, of the interwoven fabric of life. Arnold's poet is an important dimension of the "gentle stir of birth / When morning purifies the earth" (170–71) and of the "quiet trees" (173) and the "Low, woody hill, with gracious bound" (174) as he is of the populous town, though he observes its "shining streets" (167) from a distance. Yet, what is most important to him is the vital serenity of his inner life which generates and motivates his entire existence. This profound tranquillity, which will reappear in similar forms in "Stanzas in Memory of the Author of 'Obermann,'" "Empedocles on Etna," and "Stanzas from the Grande Chartreuse," is of supreme importance for Arnold. This kind of tranquillity is not merely an attribute or characteristic of an individual—rather, it is the inner strength which radiates through and emanates from his being.

Houghton and Stange in their introduction to Matthew Arnold in *Victorian Poetry and Poetics* assert Arnold's ability "to transcend a purely subjective focus by placing himself in an historical context, or seeing himself as a symbol of man in the modern world" (407). In "Resignation," in particular, Arnold's poet, by seeing himself as an integral part of the dynamic flux as well as of the "placid and continuous whole" (190) of existence, presents himself as a symbol of humanity in the modern world.

What Houghton and Stange say about Arnold's Stoic existential strategy which aspires to achieve inner calm and peace of mind in doing "what Arnold calls 'quiet work' in contrast to the battling, noisy work which is motivated by personal and worldly ambition" (405) is strikingly similar to the "gentle law" (the "sanftes Gesetz") of the mid-nineteenth-century Austrian writer Adalbert Stifter.

In the introduction to his collection of short stories, *Bunte Steine*, Stifter suggests that the calm features and quiet dimensions of nature are more noble and vital than the outwardly more conspicuous and dynamic ones:

> The blowing of the breeze, the trickling of water, the growing of grain, the surging of the sea, the greening of the earth, the sparkling of the sky, the shimmering of the stars are the things that I deem to be great. I do not consider the splendidly approaching thunderstorm, the lightning that shatters houses . . . the earthquake that chokes the land with rubble as greater than the above phenomena; in fact, I consider them less significant because they are only effects of much higher laws. (Mayer 11)

Stifter proceeds to describe the ideal life of greatness: "An entire life of justice, simplicity, self-discipline, effectiveness in one's own sphere, admiration of the beautiful . . . is the life I consider great" (14). Such a vital life is achieved by following the "gentle law," a "law" of compassion, morality, justice, and profound sensitivity. Arnold's wise tranquillity and Stifter's "gentle law" are "kindred mutations" and spiritual manifestations of one another.

Arnold's "Resignation" moves from an emphasis on the "sad lucidity of soul" (198) of the poet who observes and understands manifold aspects of the world to Fausta's notions that the poet, in his capacity to breathe "when he will, immortal air / Where Orpheus and where Homer are" (207–08), is not bound to the constraints and vicissitudes of everyday mortality. Fausta concludes her section by saying that the poet sees not deep, but wide. Though this statement is meant perhaps in a more negative than positive light, her emphasis on the breadth of vision of the poet might foreshadow the persona's attempt in "Stanzas in Memory of the Author of 'Obermann'" to gain an expansive sense of space.

Arnold's persona tells Fausta to praise, not blame, the poet, for his Stoic detachment and great sensitivity. Not only is the poet intuitively aware of the transience of passion and power, but he proceeds through life with an ease motivated by the serenity of his inner life. Arnold's persona suggests to Fausta that she and others could learn to improve their lives by following the example of the poet. The importance of the poet is affirmed not only by his "fearless mind" (244) and "rapt security" (246), as well as vital tranquillity, but also by the approval which the divine appears to confer on his existence.

This creative individual does exemplify an extraordinary understanding of and Stoic detachment from life as well as an enriching tranquillity, though he has not perhaps achieved the visionary imagination of the majestic intellect of Wordsworth's *The Prelude*. Yet, if he can "lend . . . a voice" (269), a voice of serene wisdom, to various dimensions of nature with the subtle power which Robert Browning ascribes to the subjective poet in "An Essay on Percy Bysshe Shelley," then his life will not have been in vain. Moreover, perhaps only a creative persona who has achieved a perpetually enriching serenity, a serenity which infuses his own life and radiates vitally outward, can perceive "the quiet watershed / Whence the seas of life and death are fed" (259–260) and consequently aspire to develop an expansive sense of space and time.

In "Stanzas in Memory of the Author of 'Obermann'" Arnold argues ultimately for a poetic existence which chooses neither absolute isolation nor active participation in the world but which "harmonizes" these two strategies in the dynamically productive unity (and "tension") of his own artistic vision. Obermann is an imaginary recluse in the imaginary letters of the French author Pivert de Senancour. The persona of Arnold's poem presents Obermann as an aesthetically sensitive soul who achieved an emotional-spiritual unity with nature and whose work reveals an inner torment beyond the appearance of outward calm. Obermann's introspection and extraordinary sensitivity for nature differentiate him from the society of everyday mortality. Honan describes Obermann, in his movement away from everyday society to alpine solitudes, as "a philosopher of the 'sentimental school,' who seeks an epistemology of 'feeling' and a discipline of spiritual rebirth while trying to rid himself of a tension between monkish instincts and his sense of the goodness of desire" (147–48).

Lines 41–44 of the poem elaborate on this theme of the distinction of the poet-artist from society by suggesting that while the poet may reveal certain secrets to the world he should not articulate and interpret profound mysteries of the universe because the world will not understand them. Wordsworth and Goethe represent two poets who, "in this our troubled day" (46), have attained the integrity and profundity of a vital aesthetic vision. However, the perpetual power of their poetry is somewhat diminished by the fact that Wordsworth's strategy of confronting reality has become too hermetic, too emotionally tranquil, whereas Goethe's, though outward-directed, was too isolating, too difficult to emulate. Goethe's classical tranquillity and clarity of vision is too different from the tempestuous and turbulent aura of the present.

The opening stanzas of Arnold's "Stanzas in Memory of the Author of 'Obermann'" depict the Burkean sublimity of the alpine world where Obermann once roamed. The sublimity is pervaded by an inner dynamism, for nature is in motion, especially in the first and third stanzas. The power of nature in these stanzas, exemplified by the "autumn storm-winds" (3) and the "white mists rolling" (9), is reminiscent of the vitality of the west wind in Shelley's "Ode to the West Wind."

There is an expansive sense of nature within a defined space in the opening stanzas of Arnold's poem. That the "autumn storm-winds close o'er" (3–4) the clouds, that "the abandon'd baths" (5) are "mute in their meadows lone" (6), and that "the mists are on the Rhone" (8) suggest that nature, despite its power, does not fulfill its potential for a diastolic expansiveness. Unlike the description of the mountain in Hilton's *Lost Horizon* which allows for an indefinitely open spatiality, the sense of space at the beginning of Arnold's poem is characterized by certain contours. One of these constraints on the spatial expansiveness of the mountain ambience is that Arnold's persona links the features of nature directly to a figure of mortality, to the spiritual presence of Obermann which still lingers in and affects this environment despite his physical absence.

The powerful presence of Obermann in the external landscape is reinforced by the melancholy, tempestuous spirit which radiates from his letters which the persona reads. Even the language of the poem affirms this shared influence on the persona, for the same verb, "roll," describes not only the white mists upon the sea but also the breath of Obermann's emotional vitality emerging from his letters. Arnold's persona understands Obermann's pain and the feverish energy pervading the pages of his work.

Although Obermann's work is so powerful that one sees, hears, or feels the presence of significant dimensions of nature in the process of reading, the underlying spirit of his words reveals agony and despair. One might argue that such a negative spirit, characterized and motivated by an "air of languor, cold, and death" (15) which brooded over Obermann's soul, diffuses early in the poem the possibility to develop a spatial and temporal expansiveness. Arnold's persona even wonders whether the painful focus of Obermann's work might not be a primary reason why the world has not appreciated it more.

That the persona sympathizes strongly with and appreciates Obermann is manifest not only by the assertion of an emotional-spiritual dynamism in Obermann's work and by the analogy between the vitality of Obermann's work and the power of nature but also by the persona's direct address of Obermann, calling him by name on several occasions. Moreover, after asserting the inevitable distance between the poet and the world which cannot always understand the profundity of the poet's insights, Arnold's persona places Obermann in august company, suggesting that only two other great spirits, Wordsworth and Goethe, "have attain'd / . . . to see their way" (47–48).

The chaotic tone of society ushered in and strengthened by the industrial revolution and its aftermath necessarily differentiates, Arnold's persona would suggest, his age from the Romantic period. As Arnold's persona turns his attention to the figure of Obermann he uses the phrase "the hopeless tangle of our age" (83), which in itself is a clue to the diminished potential of the post-Romantic era to aspire to and to achieve a spatial and temporal expansiveness. Obermann, "the sadder sage" (81), has expressed the Angst and inner anguish of the age, the use of the word "scann'd" (84) implying not only a capacity to view it with the luminous breadth of a Goethe but also to express one's insights creatively.

The two stanzas (lines 81–88) immediately following the description of Wordsworth and Goethe link Obermann to the two great poets. In portraying Obermann as a sage (the same word is used to apply to Goethe), though sad, Arnold's persona also claims that Obermann has the capacity to exert a spell over his readers. Lines 85–88 imply comparisons between the tranquillity of Wordsworth and that of Obermann, though Obermann's is "still / As death" (85–86), and between the differentiation from the world of Goethe and Obermann, though Obermann's is more despairing.

One might consider here Schiller's argument in "Naive and Sentimental Poetry" (1795) as a counterpoint to Arnold's understanding of Goethe. Schiller describes two types of poets, the naive, who are at one with the world, and the sentimental, who seem perpetually to be at odds with the world and draw their creative strength from such a distinction. When Schiller posits himself as an example of the sentimental poet, he sees Goethe as a paragon of the naive poet, who creates not in tension with the world of everyday mortality but in harmony with it.

The tension within the poet between the urge to participate in the world and the desire for solitude represents the tension in Arnold's persona as well. For, as is suggested in Arnold's "Resignation," the poet should develop a strategy of Stoic detachment with respect to the world of everyday mortality. In line 97 Arnold's persona raises the question where the thrill of life is to be found—his answer is that it is not to be discovered in the world or in the strife of man. Instead, the thrill of life is to be found in an approach to life which emphasizes participation in life without the loss of the self, stressing the notion of being in life but not of it. Arnold's persona resolves this tension temporarily by returning to his contemplation of the alpine landscape.

The creative power which the persona ascribes to Obermann is evident not only in the persona's address of Obermann as sage and seer, but also in the association of Obermann with the vitality of the alpine landscape. For example, in lines 109–112 the persona speaks of Obermann as having pleasures to share with those who come to his ambience, namely "Balms floating on thy mountain-air / And healing sights to see" (111–12). As the depiction of the mountain environment progresses, Obermann assumes the qualities of a nature-spirit as vital as the spirit of autumn in Keats' "Ode to Autumn."

Obermann's powers as a nature-spirit, as a presence in nature and of nature, are described as especially visual (lines 115–23) and auditory (lines 124–28). The moment that portrays Obermann's presence in nature is a threshold moment—Arnold's persona depicts Obermann watching "The summer-day grow late" (116) and "darkness steal o'er the wet grass / With the pale crocus starr'd" (117–18). In presenting Obermann at this moment of evening, perhaps Arnold's persona suggests that Obermann's capacity as a nature-spirit to appreciate sensitively the revelation of both day and night is stimulated by the threshold nature of this experience. Obermann does achieve a sense of spatial expansiveness of soul here through his powerful vision because it extends to the contours of this alpine ambience, to the waters of Lake Leman below and to the "distant peaks of snow" (123).

In the aura of night Obermann hears "accents of the eternal tongue" (125) playing through the pine branches and as a result is rejuvenated. As in Wordsworth's *The Prelude*, so in Arnold's "Stanzas in Memory of the Author of 'Obermann'" space precedes time, in that the potential expansiveness of space is explored as a prelude to the concern with the potential expansiveness of time. Unlike Empedocles, who must redissolve himself in nature to renew the self, Obermann exists, in the spirit of Schiller's naive poet, in a unified, harmonious relation with nature. The capacity of Obermann to revitalize himself by hearing "accents of the eternal tongue" (125) playing through the pine branches suggests his participation in the expansiveness of time. This statement is less powerful and less comprehensive than the assertion of Wordsworth's majestic intellect in *The Prelude* that he can hold fit converse not only with the spiritual world but also with past, present, and future generations of humankind until Time shall no longer exist. For Wordsworth's persona participates directly in and perhaps even shapes the openendedness of time while claiming the ultimate cessation of mortality, whereas Arnold's persona, though he feels temporarily revitalized, does not assert the end of time.

Perhaps the inability to make such a sweeping, powerful claim compels Arnold's persona to listen to the accents of the eternal tongue and then to weep. Of course, it is a tribute to Obermann's nature-sensibility that he can hear the accents of the eternal tongue—the melodies of the eternal spirit of nature—for only a sage or seer would be capable of such an achievement. Yet, the introduction of "wept" (128) into this aura of potential eternity suggests the immanence of mortality behind the transient revitalization of the self.

With the word "wept" comes also the separation of Arnold's persona from the direct healing qualities of this mountain ambience. For in the next lines (lines 129–32) he asserts not only that such dreams of the eternal melody of nature may deceive but also that fate drives him onward. Unlike Obermann (and, by implication, Senancour) and Wordsworth, Arnold's persona is not possessed of the tranquillity which can encourage and enable the individual to sit "By some high chalet-door" (115) and watch "The summer-day grow late" (116). Arnold's persona cannot control or shape his destiny as can those who are motivated and pervaded by a Buddha-like serenity. Yet, even though Arnold's persona feels compelled by fate to move on, he acknowledges that he leaves a considerable part of himself in the mountain ambience.

After implying in lines 133–36 that he is subject to the caprices of fate as an "unknown Power" (133), this persona proclaims that he must live in the world, that he cannot exist in the condition of almost absolute isolation from the ambience of everyday mortality in which the "melancholy shade" (138), Obermann, resides. It is interesting to note here that as the poem progresses Arnold's persona ceases to call his spiritual companion "Obermann" and instead addresses him in a series of phrases that highlight Obermann's essential features as a creator and nature-spirit. If one considers lines 137ff. as an indication of the attitude of Arnold's persona towards Obermann, then this shift in naming should not be construed in a negative light. For although Arnold's persona cannot live in this secluded mountain environment, he shows more envy and respect than negative feelings towards Obermann for being able to do so. Indeed, Arnold's persona even asks Obermann not to condemn or upbraid him for being unable and unwilling to achieve Obermann's supreme nature-sensibility and his participation in the realm of "the Children of the Second Birth" (143).

The spatial expansiveness of Obermann, implied in lines 115–23, is affirmed in lines 141–52. Arnold's persona says that Obermann, who, in the vitality of his nature-presence, has achieved the spiritual strength to be in the world but not of it, has "gone away from earth" (141), has liberated himself from the spatial parameters of mortality. Obermann's spirit belongs to the world of the "Children of the Second Birth" (143), whom the world could not tame. These are individuals who have not immersed and lost themselves in the commotion and disorder of the world of transience (a danger of which Arnold speaks in "Resignation"), nor have they been tainted by the world.

As hermetic and isolating as the experience of Obermann in the alpine solitudes seems to be, the ultimate goal of this nature-spirit is an existence deriving its vitality from the complementary features of a strong sensitivity for nature and of a sense of community with likeminded souls. The significance of this community derives from the fact that these individuals who have liberated themselves from the fetters of a materialistic world-view devoted to aggressive competition, and inspired by the "progress" of the industrial revolution and who have tried to create a climate of existence where the socio-economic distinction which pervade the domain of transience and give it substance and form no longer exist.

In saying farewell to the spirit of Obermann in the alpine landscape, Arnold's persona encompasses in himself some of the qualities which he emphasizes as crucial to the significance of this nature-soul. Arnold's persona, by describing the capacity for diastolic spatiality and temporality in Obermann, absorbs in himself (or infuses himself with) a semblance of such capacity as well. Not only does Arnold's persona reveal ultimately the melancholy and sadness which he ascribed to Obermann, but he seems to exhibit a sense of spatial expansiveness in the last few stanzas as well.

Yet, the sense of spatial expansiveness is diminished by the inevitable presence of mortality, designated by such images as the moss-grown date on the grave and the necessity of having it cleared periodically as well as the image of the "hardly-heard-of grave" (180). One might say that the images of mortality transform the expansive spatiality to a centripetal sense of space. The centripetal, inward-directed spatiality of the images is reinforced at the end by the well-defined boundaries and contours in the descriptions of space. In its ultimate emphasis on centripetal spatiality and hermetic temporality (especially in the last stanza) "Stanzas in Memory of the Author of 'Obermann'" anticipates and foreshadows the experience of space and time in "Empedocles on Etna."

Neiman claims in *Matthew Arnold* that the only viable strategy for the aesthetically and intellectually aware individual of 1849, according to Arnold, is "a stoic demeanor dramatized by Obermann's retreat into an Alpine hermitage where he is a kind of Byronic scholar-gipsy" (65). The inner tension of the poetic persona who wishes to participate in the world to gain a more insightful understanding of it and to differentiate himself from the mortal vicissitudes of such a world is reinforced by the last few stanzas which imply that the Obermann-like figure could be buried either in an aura of hermetic isolation near Lake Geneva or in an ambience of orphic plenitude near Paris. Of this poem Edward Alexander writes that it expands a paradox previously presented in "Resignation": "Here as in the earlier poem we are told that the poet can see the world more clearly and fully as a detached spectator than as a committed participant; but here we are also told that only in solitude and isolation from the world can joy be found" (63).

This inner tension is perhaps exacerbated by the fact that nature is not a completely healing force. Douglas Bush writes of the healing power of nature: "Arnold's temperamental idealism is inevitably kept in check by modern rationalism; and his attitudes toward nature—or Nature—are variable, within or sometimes outside the major premise. Of course such a lover of streams and flowers is fully open to the healing power of the beauties of earth, but that is limited and occasional and only mitigates the 'groundtone / Of human agony'" (43). The healing power of nature can perhaps not assuage the "unstrung will" (183) and the "broken heart" (183). That "broken heart" (183) rhymes with "part" (181) intensifies the emotional anguish of the farewell scenario. Yet, the rhyming of "dell" (182) and "farewell" (184) suggests that though the persona will leave the hermetic tranquillity of Obermann's world there will remain, as in Eichendorff's "Abschied," a permanent spiritual link between them, that part of his soul will always be among the "Balms floating on the mountain-air" (111) and will always be listening to the "accents of the eternal tongue" (125) playing through the pine branches.

"Empedocles on Etna" articulates a poetic existence informed by a painfully profound tension similar to that in "Stanzas in Memory of the Author of 'Obermann.'" Empedocles is a sage who lives isolated from the world and who is weary of solitude and of a condition of reality which disdains or misunderstands him. He wants to liberate himself from his solitude, yet he does not want to lose his individuality. Thus, this poetic persona, as Thomas Mann's protagonist in *Tonio Kröger*, is caught between two worlds and is at home in neither. Unlike Mann's protagonist who resolves the tension at least symbolically in his devotion to artistic, literary activity, Empedocles, however, resolves the tension in his longing for the abyss and for death (for a union of the self and nature).

Empedocles wants to feel the emotional and spiritual closeness to nature which Wordsworth's persona experiences in "Tintern Abbey"—he yearns to experience the sense sublime of a creative individual in a state of emotional and spiritual unity and totality with nature. However, Empedocles seems to be destined to fulfill a painful fate, for not only is he disdained by the world of everyday mortality, but he is also disappointed in the actions of Apollo, one of the gods, if not the god, who should symbolize a positive source of his poetic inspiration.

Joseph Carroll in *The Cultural Theory of Matthew Arnold* says that "Empedocles on Etna" is "Arnold's most thorough exploration of the spiritual malaise of his own times" (2). He suggests that Arnold repudiates this poem because the suffering of Empedocles finds no active, affirmative resolution. Carroll writes that for Arnold "the age of Empedocles, the declining period of Greece, serves as a prototype for post-Christian Europe. Like the age of Empedocles, Arnold's own modern age is marked by the doubt, discouragement, and self-involved intellectuality of Hamlet and Faust" (2).

Carroll argues further that the primary source of Empedocles' despair is that "he cannot find any relation between these elements of life and the activity of the mind" (7). When Empedocles realizes, as Carroll asserts, that "there is no possibility of union between the animated life of nature and the divisive, intrusive, and distorted character of the intellect" (7), then his plunge into the crater seems inevitable. Perhaps Empedocles' plunge into the crater represents a kind of experience of expansive spatiality because he does achieve a dissolution of the self in nature.

Carroll suggests that Arnold, unlike Empedocles, is able to overcome, at least to some extent, his despair:

He overcomes despair by overcoming the causes of Empedocles' plight—the division of mind and nature and the consequent sense of futility in the cultural progression. In the critical effort that culminates in *Culture and Anarchy* Arnold will profess a creed that synthesizes the rationalist ideal of a complete and unified consciousness with a progressivist scheme of historical development. (14–15)

Arnold, unlike Empedocles, is able to transform the negative into the positive Weltanschauung of Carlyle's Teufelsdrockh. Though Arnold does not share Carlyle's conviction in the inevitably progressive development of history, his personae in "Stanzas in Memory of the Author of 'Obermann'" and in "Stanzas from the Grande Chartreuse" especially do represent heroic figures in the sense that they understand intuitively the divine idea of the universe.

Although Empedocles is weary of solitude, he needs it for the development of his creative vitality. Yet, he acknowledges at the same time that he finds solitude too painful sometimes as well. His existence becomes, thus, a perpetual Heraclitean shifting from one realm of thought and activity to another, from the self-encompassing, self-suffusing, self-tormenting solitude of the creative artist to the self-challenging chaos of everyday mortality.

Warren Anderson describes the alternatives of "Empedocles on Etna," the interaction and tension of which constitute the central dilemma of the poem: "The Empedoclean-Pausanian mind, the mind of the modern intellectual, turns from an infected world inward upon itself and scorns away other recourse. Callicles, symbol of the classical ideal expressed through its most perfect medium, accepts the world around him as sound and beautiful" (38). Edward Alexander reinforces Anderson's description of the Empedoclean mind when he writes of the plight of Empedocles: "Arnold, like Ruskin, found that the disinterested effort to see things as they really are and then to describe what one sees causes that disinterested seer to become isolated from his fellow men" (87).

In an attempt to resolve or to reconcile himself to his profound isolation, Empedocles finds the possibility of salvation (with perhaps a semblance of spatial and temporal expansiveness) in an intense participation in nature. In Act II he exclaims:

Oh, that I could glow like this mountain!
Oh, that my heart bounded with the swell of sea!
Oh, that my soul were full of light as the stars!
Oh, that it brooded over the world like the air! (323–26)

In these lines Empedocles reveals a dynamic longing to be infused with the power of nature almost as powerful as that of Shelley's persona in "Ode to the West Wind." The crucial difference between the two personae is that Shelley's reveals a confidence, which Empedocles does not, not only in his capacity to participate intensely in nature, in the inner power and beauty of nature, but also in his conviction in the importance of his own creative endeavors.

Yet, at his dying moment Empedocles asserts the vitality of his existence in that he has pursued consistently the ideal of an independence of spirit and freedom of the soul while loving no darkness, sophisticating no truth, nursing no delusion, and allowing no fear. This is a heroic gesture which gives the character and existence of Empedocles a provisional nobility. In the final lines before he plunges into the crater Empedocles affirms that this Stoic devotion to certain humanitarian ideals has preserved the integrity of his soul—however, ultimately he breathes freely only for a moment before his escape into the abyss. The final moment is an experience of epiphanic energy in which the soul of Empedocles glows to meet the spirit of nature before plunging into the abyss.

Honan stresses the affirmative tone of the final action of Empedocles: "Clouded and oppressed, he was still capable of intelligent action, and his suicidal leap into Mt. Etna's crater was affirmative. It was an action such as honest Rene on Mt. Etna, or even the joy-seeking Obermann in the Alps might take" (184). Honan argues further that Empedocles, by reuniting himself with the universe in his death-scenario, "would remain young and 'human' forever" (184). Perhaps only by reuniting himself with the universe can Empedocles achieve a semblance of spatial and temporal expansiveness, as transient as it may be.

Alan Roper in *Arnold's Poetic Landscapes* says that Empedocles commits suicide "while he can still feel at one with himself and with the whole world; while he can still hope to escape the dreary cycle of metempsychosis through ever more fruitless lives" (186). Roper continues to assert that "Empedocles on Etna" differs noticeably from previous, similar poems dealing with the interaction of humankind and the natural world "by being about a man who has, or had, a philosophy of the oneness of man and natural phenomena" (188). The personae in "Stanzas in Memory of the Author of 'Obermann'" and in "Stanzas from the Grande Chartreuse" do seem to have a unified vision of humankind and natural phenomena, but it is more hermetic and eclectic than that of Empedocles. Moreover, they have a sense of their own emotional and intellectual unity which perhaps enhances their capacity to develop and sustain a unified vision. Perhaps Empedocles must lose the self, must dissolve it in nature before he can regain it. For he does describe himself at the end as being far from his own soul. Moreover, the physical dissolution of the self in nature will produce a spiritual catharsis and liberation.

Empedocles is such an important figure because he symbolizes the struggle of the individual in contemporary society for integrity and vitality. The divisive influences in Empedocles represent also Arnold's personal crises:

> Here Arnold's dismal privately confessed 'spiritual lethargy' and 'strain and uneasiness,' his sense of London as a desert and his headaches and worries over a sister's engagement mingle in a panorama in which the living are dead, and a dead father . . . is alive but powerless. (Honan 203)

The industrialized "landscape of the European soul in its busy, brittle, hollow age of disbelief" (Honan 203) only exacerbates the inner conflicts and tensions which confront and engage Empedocles in his quest for a revitalization of the self.

In "Stanzas from the Grande Chartreuse" Arnold portrays a persona who does achieve a serene wisdom and spiritual tranquillity in a space of hermetic spatiality. In September 1851, Arnold himself visited the monastery of the Grande Chartreuse, where he saw not only the library, chapel, and cloisters, but was given a cell to sleep in. Honan argues that for Arnold "the Roman Catholic faith, though unpurged as he felt from inadmissible features of doctrine and dogma, was one measure of the adequacy of a world outlook" (240). Moreover, Arnold sensed that an age of faith comparable to the unified vision of the Middle Ages might reemerge in the future to assuage the restlessness and anguish caused by a mechanical, excessive rationalism (240).

The first stanza of "Stanzas from the Grande Chartreuse" describes the diversity of the landscape through which the persona must travel. In contrast to the upward motion of the first stanza, the second stanza presents a downward-looking perspective: while in the first stanza the persona looks up the mountainside, in the second he gazes down into the cauldron of vapors. The transformation of the placid aura of stanza one to the terrifying aura of stanza two is suggested as well by the description of the rain, which suffuses the meadow softly in stanza one, but becomes a driving force of increasingly more powerful proportions as the evening darkens. J. M. W. Turner's watercolor *Lake*

Lucerne: the Bay of Uri from above Brunnen (1842) reveals an ambience similar to the one described at the opening of Arnold's poem. The cauldron of vapors in the middle of the watercolor, suffusing both the lake and the mountain, clears slightly at the edge of land and sea to affirm a moment of tranquillity.

In stanzas three and four the gaze of the persona is once more directed upward into the atmosphere of the Burkean sublime which pervades this mountain landscape. The perception of buildings beyond the spectral vapors is similar to the conception of structures through and beyond the mountain mists in Turner's watercolor *Goldau with the Lake of Zug in the Distance* (1841–42). In both works the inspirational edifice appears through "the showery twilight grey" (22).

One might compare the passage up the mountainside of Arnold's persona with Turner's watercolor *Glacier and Source of the Arveiron* (1803). The slanting line of the mountainside is the oblique line which may rise to infinity which Turner discusses in his lectures. Of this work Wilton writes: "It links the placid tranquillity of the valley with the harsh energy of the cloudy peaks, and imbues the whole design with the unsteady rhythm of the rocky, unsure goat-paths and the avalanche-invaded forest" (121). This moment represents the stage of the spectral vapors which encompass and rush by the persona.

The final stage of the ascent of Arnold's persona finds a painterly analogue in Turner's engraving *Llanthony Abbey* (1836) which reveals a seemingly spectral or unearthly edifice beyond the mountain precipice and torrents. The pervasively misty aura of this work is not present in Turner's 1794 watercolor of Llanthony Abbey. In this work the abbey, though a ruin, appears beyond the lingering clouds and vapors of the heights as a sublime revelation in the mountain landscape. Turner's *Llanthony Abbey* (1836) and Arnold's Grande Chartreuse are both permeated by an etherial tranquillity which generates the vitality not only of the structure itself but also of the surrounding landscape. Turner's Llanthony Abbey and Arnold's Grande Chartreuse are so intimately linked by color, form, and aura to the surrounding landscape that they appear to be emanations of it.

The white of the "spectral vapours" (13) rushing past "limestone scars with ragged pines" (14) is revived in the "gleaming white" (36) of the "cowl'd forms" (36). Yet, as ghostlike as these "cowl'd forms" (36) are in the night they are differentiated from the white of the vapours by the gleam which radiates from them. Although the courts are described as silent, this should not suggest an aura of lifelessness, for these courts contain "splashing icy fountains" (33) which are perhaps the source for the mountain torrents. The silent courts, as the features of the mountainside described in the persona's ascent, represent a hermetic sense of space. Each of the landscape features appears hermetic and self-contained—each has its place and does not try to expand into another sphere of existence.

Likewise, the silent courts seem to be content to participate in a cyclical ritual where the icy fountains splash water into their stone-carved basins. This ritual is meant to be considered less stagnant than dynamic. Though it occurs "night and day" (31), suggesting that it follows the temporality of mortality, the fact that it represents a seemingly perpetual cycle of renewal implies that it is also beyond the constraints of time. And although the courts are silent, this is a silence of inner vitality, for not only does it encompass the movements of gleaming white figures but it signifies the energy-source of the monastery and of the mountain cascades. The water participates in an orderly cycle moving from fountain to basin and back again while at the same time having the capacity to transcend these limits, as the image of the humid corridors suggests. Yet, ultimately the silent courts as well as the fountains and cowled forms appear to represent and reinforce a hermetic, not an outward-directed, sense of space.

Lines 43–48 affirm the seemingly hermetic nature of this space. After participating in the chapel ritual of "passing the Host from hand to hand" (42), the pale visage of each monk "is buried in his cowl once more" (44). Each monastic cell has an aura of hermetic vitality and suffering which is intensified by the image of the wooden bed as a place for daily rest and as a final resting-place.

Arnold describes the library also as a space of hermetic strength leading to decay. The tracts and tomes of the library are not to "feed priestly pride" (50), nor to "hymn the conquering march of Rome" (51), nor to amuse, but rather to "paint of souls the inner strife" (53). The hermetic strategy of this lifestyle is infused with pain and penitential cries, for these individuals have died to life. Arnold's persona considers these places to be characterized to some extent by physical decay and by an absence of growth, perhaps necessary prerequisites to spiritual improvement and stimulation. Yet, it is not clear—for Arnold does not even seem to imply it—that physical suffering entails or leads to spiritual growth. However, if we think of the necessity of some protagonists in nineteenth- and twentieth-century literature (in Thomas Mann's work, for example) to die to life in order to create vitally, perhaps this notion is not as negative as it might seem to be.

The possibility of growth is introduced by the image of the garden in line 55. Though overgrown, this secret garden is mild, in contrast to the austerity and severity of the chapel and library, and possesses flowering fragrant herbs. The tone of the stanza which describes the monks' gardening task differs considerably from that of the previous stanzas which are permeated by an aura of pain and decay. Moreover, this cheerful labor is performed beyond the parameters, whether considered limiting or not, of the monastic cells. That this labor, their one human task, is achieved outdoors "beneath the sun" (60) implies the capacity of expansiveness, though it is not directly nurtured.

After this brief interlude which presents a view of nature more mild and domestic than the tempestuous sense of nature developed in the opening stanzas of the poem, Arnold's persona asserts the international breadth of the monastic brotherhood at the Grande Chartreuse. In saying that he perceives the "pilgrim-hosts of old" (62) in these halls, Arnold's persona asserts his own conceptual capability to transcend the immediate temporal context. This statement also emphasizes the temporal continuity of the Grande Chartreuse, a monastic culture that can exist through the flux of time.

In the next few stanzas starting with line 67, Arnold's persona responds to the question the teachers of his youth whisper to him: "What dost thou in this living tomb" (72)? He responds to these teachers, who, in the spirit of the Enlightenment, aspired to truth along the path of fact and reason, by saying that he did not come to the Grande Chartreuse to be their enemy and to deny their teaching, but rather to revitalize his spirit in the seclusion of this monastery.

In describing himself as "Wandering between two worlds, one dead / The other powerless to be born" (85–86), Arnold's persona exemplifies the metaphysical tension not only of the author himself but also of the Victorian age. This metaphysical tension is grounded in the isolation, restlessness, frustration about the anguish of existence, and a melancholic longing for an earlier age of peace, faith, and moral integrity (an age perhaps both perceived and imaginatively constructed). Arnold's persona affirms these aspects of the metaphysical tension from line 85, first revealing a restlessness deriving from his sense of wandering between two worlds without feeling at home in either. Moreover, he can find no place of tranquillity: "With nowhere yet to rest my head / Like these, on earth I wait forlorn" (87–88). Unlike some of the Romantic poets who derived at least some of their creative strength from a restlessness of spirit and from a profound Wanderlust, Arnold wants to liberate himself from this restlessness to achieve a sense of rich serenity.

Carroll suggests that in "Stanzas from the Grande Chartreuse" Arnold portrays "his own dramatic effort to overcome or mitigate this distress and despair by transforming the faith he has lost into an object of aesthetic contemplation" (25). Arnold, like the persona of the poem, undertook a journey to the Carthusian monastery near Grenoble so that he could possess his soul again. Carroll states that Arnold "has sought out the monastery so that he may use its atmosphere of penitential withdrawal to stimulate within himself a fantasy world of peaceful meditation" (26).

Because the penitential exercises of the Carthusians may be seen as actions to attain salvation, Arnold, in going to the monastery, "is attempting to cultivate in himself an aesthetic appreciation of a moral grandeur that can no longer be part of a living world for him" (Carroll 26). By turning inward in a hermetic gesture which disengages the mind from the external world of everyday mortality, Arnold's persona shows a contentment with a contoured sense of space and time. He is interested not in transcendence or expansiveness, but in the sublime, revitalizing seclusion which the tranquillity of the Grande Chartreuse offers.

The quietude of sensibility of this monastic environment is not to be found in the chaotic, tempestuous world of everyday mortality which only disdains the tears of Arnold's persona. In contrast to the insensitive and thoughtless world of everyday mortality, the Grande Chartreuse offers a space for the profound renewal of the soul. In apostrophizing the ambience of the Grande Chartreuse to conceal him in its "gloom profound" (91), the persona claims the need for a sanctuary where he can not only revitalize his soul but also free his thoughts from their transient burdens.

The criticism of the arena of transience by Arnold's persona is heightened in lines 97–102—in critiquing the world's inability to understand the faith of the Church or his own melancholy, Arnold's persona intensifies the differentiation which he feels so intensely from the world of everyday mortality. In a letter to A. H. Clough in May 1850, Arnold expresses his concern that the world does not understand faith:

> The world in general has always stood towards religions and their doctors in the attitude of a half-astonished clown acquiescingly ducking at their grand words and thinking it must be very fine, but for its soul not being able to make out what it is all about. (Houghton and Stange, 477)

Arnold expresses effectively his concern about the lack of emotional sensitivity in the external world in his poem "Memorial Verses" where he criticizes the era of doubts and disputes as incapable of appreciating the importance of Wordsworth's healing power.

The apocalyptic undertone of the next two stanzas is reminiscent of the metaphysical despair pervading the existence of Empedocles, who, perhaps because he has lost a sense of serenity so vital to the presentation of the creative persona in "Resignation," can only confront his restless despair in the dissolution of the self. The apocalyptic undertone in "Stanzas from the Grande Chartreuse" is especially evident in the lines:

> But—if you cannot give us ease—
> Last of the race of them who grieve
> Here leave us to die out with these
> Last of the people who believe. (109–12)

The persona in "Stanzas from the Grande Chartreuse" anticipates the ending to an age of doubt and despair, and is able to preserve a sense of self in the tranquillity of the monastic sanctuary.

L. R. Pratt emphasizes the revitalizing power of the Grande Chartreuse in her essay "Matthew Arnold and the Modernist Image": "In contrast to 'Lines Written in Kensington Gardens' Arnold finds in his images of the Grande Chartreuse a powerful emotional resolution" (87). Pratt proceeds to argue that "Arnold's image of the Grande Chartreuse provides a setting . . . to give tragic dignity to his tears, and to reaffirm the inevitability of his alienation from the modern world" (87–88).

Pratt continues her argument by making an interesting comparison between Arnold and Yeats:

> The image of the Grande Chartreuse parallels in function Yeats' city of Byzantium, the Tower, or the wild swans at Coole. Both poets use images to create moments of emotional release under aesthetic control, moments that synthesize the material world with the inner life. (88)

This important point suggests that the hermetic approach which Arnold's persona adopts in this poem does not have to be construed in negative terms. In other words, because the persona turns inward and does not show an interest in developing an expansive sense of space and time is not a negative achievement. As long as the persona who chooses the hermetic strategy is content with the vitality of such an experience, whether the focus is emotional, spiritual, intellectual, or a combination thereof, the experience should be considered as affirmative. Arnold's persona in fact asserts that the emotional vitality which he preserves in the ambience of the Grande Chartreuse is not appreciated by the external world of everyday mortality, suggesting that the aura of the Grande Chartreuse is more emotionally, spiritually, and imaginatively vital then one might be led to believe.

As Hilton's protagonist in *Lost Horizon*, Arnold's persona in "Stanzas from the Grande Chartreuse" believes in the importance of a sanctuary of emotional and spiritual vitality away from the chaotic, unappreciative, insensitive world of transience. However, whereas Arnold's persona is content with the inevitability of silence as a final solution, which is thoroughly inward-looking without a concern for or conviction in the future, Hilton's protagonist believes in the significance of Shangri-La as a sanctuary for the emotional, spiritual, and intellectual vitality of the sensitive individual and of civilization, a place containing the cultural seeds of the future.

In lines 115–26 Arnold's persona laments the loss of feeling which has pervaded the contemporary world—in contrasting this lack of emotional sensitivity in the present age to the emotional vitality of the Romantic period, Arnold's persona reinforces the nostalgic, backward-looking, inward-directed approach which motivates his existence. The anguish of the present generation, suggests Arnold, is only intensified by the fact that though the sufferers of the previous generation have passed away, not only have "they left their pain" (131), but "the pangs which tortured them remain" (132). The passage of time does not enhance the possibilities of emotional, spiritual growth—instead, such possibilities are thwarted in the cycle of pain which the flux of time necessitates and strengthens.

Time is not a healer in this poem as it is for such contemporary works as Dickens' *David Copperfield* or Eliot's *Middlemarch*. While David and Dorothea are able to overcome and resolve their respective difficulties in the passage of time, Arnold's persona is not able to, only suspending the anguish of the present age by retreating to a sanctuary of peace. Perhaps Arnold's persona is less able to resolve his tensions because, unlike his contemporary literary protagonists David and Dorothea, he sees himself less as an individual than as a symbol of his times. Dorothea, too, sees herself as symbolic of a new creative potential in women, but she is less undermined by the melancholic despair that permeates Arnold's persona.

The despair of Arnold's persona, which seems to be hermetic and present- or past-directed for most of the poem, is modified only slightly in lines 157–62 where the possibility of a new age of greater sensibility in the future is raised. Yet, Arnold's persona is not confident of the realization of this possibility, especially because the present age seems so disdainful of or incapable of appreciating the struggles of writers such as Byron and Shelley. The Europe of Byron's age "made his woe her own" (138), yet the Europe of mid-century, Arnold's persona suggests, does not sense the importance of the achievement and sacrifice of Byron, Shelley, and other similarly vital literary figures.

Arnold's persona hopes that a new, more emotionally and culturally dynamic age will emerge which will be wise without hardness and "gay without frivolity" (160). While he waits for such an age to dawn, Arnold's persona implores the world to allow his tears of hope and anguish. That Arnold's persona apostrophizes the world here is interesting because it suggests that he has not differentiated himself as clearly from the world of everyday mortality as was implied earlier in the poem. For if he had distinguished himself more vitally from the external world, then he would perhaps not need to ask such a world to allow his tears. Or perhaps he is asking the external world to allow his tears in the sense that he is trying to encourage the world to develop its emotional sensitivity, though he senses that it will not follow his example.

Arnold's persona proceeds to praise the world, expressing his admiration for the power and vitality of the world of everyday mortality which not only gives the universe a law but which also triumphs over time and space. In concluding this stanza with the statement that though he praises these features of the world, "they are not ours" (168), Arnold's persona suggests two important points: first, that he ultimately does differentiate himself from the world of transience, and, second, that he feels enough of a sense of unity with the ambience of the Grande Chartreuse to use "ours" to fuse his view and that of the monastic world.

It seems as if Arnold's persona is suggesting that the world of everyday transience should be praised on its own merits, just as the domain of the Grande Chartreuse should be praised on its own strengths. The world of everyday mortality may give the universe a law, but it is its own law and not a universal law of existence. Moreover, the world of transience may triumph over time and space, but its temporal and spatial contours and the spatial and temporal parameters over which it triumphs are different from those of the Grande Chartreuse, which creates its own realm of spatial and temporal vitality.

In line 169 Arnold's persona reaffirms the hermetic nature of the Grande Chartreuse ambience and of those who appreciate its tranquillity intuitively:

> We are like children rear'd in shade
> Beneath some old-world abbey wall,
> Forgotten in a forest-glade,
> And secret from the eyes of all. (169–72)

This environment is not only sheltered but it is also forgotten: the abbey and the surrounding forest signify a world of its own. The hermetic vitality of this world, similar to the hermetic dynamism of Samuel Palmer's *In a Shoreham Garden* (1829), is strengthened by the underlying energy of the aura of the Grande Chartreuse. For, though the individuals of this monastic world appear to be forgotten in a forest-glade, "Deep, deep the greenwood round them waves" (173).

The individual walking so serenely through the garden in Palmer's *In a Shoreham Garden* exudes an etherial, otherworldly tranquillity which characterizes Arnold's persona in the Grande Chartreuse ambience as well. As Arnold's persona, Palmer's figure seems to be "forgotten in a forest-glade" (171) and "secret from the eyes of all" (172), and yet, both individuals participate in a growth process too subtle to be appreciated by the world of everyday mortality. As nature is the source of the underlying vitality of Palmer's garden, so it is for the Grande Chartreuse, as is implied by stanzas six through ten of Arnold's poem—the aura of decay and shadow of the silent courts and library is complemented by the subtle burgeoning of the garden outside.

The rhyme-scheme of this stanza (lines 169–74) reinforces the hermetic nature of this extraordinary space. "Shade" (169) and "glade" (171) reaffirm the hermetic ambience as do "waves" and "graves" (174). The verbal energy of "waves" spills over into the alliteration of "greenwood" (173) and "graves," fusing these complementary images into a coherent whole. Yet, the end-rhymes of lines 2 and 4 might seem to challenge this centripetal strategy, for whereas "wall" (170) affirms the hermetic nature of this context, "all" (172), suggesting the presence of the outside world, challenges it. Though Arnold's persona asserts that this forest-glade is "secret from the eyes of all" (172), perhaps those eyes are just as able as the eyes which penetrate the sanctuary of Palmer's Shoreham Garden to perceive the activity of the Grande Chartreuse.

The possibility of such visual encroachment, of a disturbance of the etherial quietude of the monastic ambience is elaborated upon in the next stanza where "passing troops" (177) can be glimpsed through the trees. The "passing troops" in this stanza and the "hunters" (183) and "gay dames" (185) of the next symbolize the energy, passion, and tumult which the world of "tireless powers" (167) offers. Although the "bugle-music on the breeze" (189) seems to address the hermetic individuals as well, these "children rear'd in shade" (169) will not respond, not only because they have been called too late, but also because they perhaps do not even want to be called at all. For individuals who share Arnold's belief in the importance of achieving a profound serenity and wisdom in addition to a Stoic detachment from the world would not instinctively be interested in the fanfare and noise of the world of transience.

In the last two stanzas the attention shifts once more from interruptions of the outside world to the context of the hermetic space. The individuals reared "Beneath some old-world abbey wall" (170) reply to the fanfare of the outside world by turning inward to the eternal present of the cloister, which reveals not only "emblems of hope over the grave" (201) but also organ-melodies "of another sphere" (204). The arrangement of these two images is reminiscent of the structural pattern of two similar images in "Stanzas in Memory of the Author of 'Obermann'." In both poems there is a coupling of an inspirational image of height (the rosy light fading from the peaks of snow in the one is analogous to the shining of yellow tapers in the high altar's divine depth in the other) which directly precedes an image of etherial sound ("the accents of the eternal tongue" playing through the pine branches in the one is comparable to the organ "accents of another sphere" in the other). Though the rosy light of "Stanzas in Memory of the Author of 'Obermann'" fades into night, the "light"-"night" end-rhyme suggests that this motion represents less a differentiation than a fusion. The rosy light, like the yellow tapers of "Stanzas from the Grande Chartreuse," signifies an emblem of hope over the grave.

Perhaps the main reason why the organ-tones of the Grande Chartreuse do not offer the same potential for renewal as the "accents of the eternal tongue" in the pine branches is that they have been constrained in the "cloistral round" (205), whereas the others have blossomed and developed in the expansive space of nature. Yet, although

Arnold's persona implies the stagnant stability of the monastic ambience which is not overtly growth-oriented and although he describes
this ambience as a "desert" (210), one should not interpret these statements as primarily critical of the Grande Chartreuse. For the monastery has a self-imposed responsibility to distinguish itself from the world
of everyday mortality which, unlike the cloister, is less inclined to achieve
an aura of serenity and quiet wisdom. "Desert" (210) may suggest the
perils to cultural vitality of excessive isolation of the Grande Chartreuse, but this is still an ambience in which active verbs of growth
("grow" in line 207 and "flower" in line 208) apply.

Honan asserts that in the final stanzas "the Grande Chartreuse
becomes a more manageable, personal symbol" (241) suggesting the
security of childhood. Honan proceeds to claim that "the Stoic spirit
of Epictetus and the rational spirit of Voltaire brood over the end of
the poem" (242). The departure of Arnold's persona from the monastic world is imminent when he fuses the Stoic and rational inclinations
in his character in expressing his belief in the importance of genuinely
vital moral action.

Arnold's persona will leave the ambience of the Grande Chartreuse
having completed his quest for the "magic mountain." He has been
emotionally and spiritually rejuvenated by the sanctuary of the cloister, but he realizes, perhaps most intensely through his experience of
the hermetic sense of time and space, that he must return to the world
below. For Arnold's ideal is to be in the world of everyday life without
being of it. The "magic mountain" experience has given a "spot of
time" which will perpetually nourish his soul. Yet, it has also intensified his own inner metaphysical tension.

On the one hand, the experience of the Grande Chartreuse, which
reveals the home of the "last of the people who believe" (112), represents an ultimate vision, or sense, of tranquillity and of stoically wise
detachment from the world of everyday mortality. This experience of
tranquillity is at the same time an experience of existential tension for
the poet "Wandering between two worlds, one dead / The other powerless to be born" (85–86). Such tranquillity can only be temporary,
for the poet, whose creativity is generated at least to some extent by
the metaphysical tension, must express the despair of what Allott calls
"the lost generation of the later 1840s" (xxii), which suffered from the
"seismic shocks caused by the religious, political, and social upheav-
als" (xxii) and encompassed the "permanent casualties of the sensitive
and reflective" (xxii).

As Mann's Castorp in *The Magic Mountain*, Arnold's persona feels he must return to the "flatland" below to contribute most effectively to the improvement of the world. Unlike Castorp, who sacrifices himself in the war with a pointlessness of which the author himself does not seem fully aware, Arnold's persona will return to engage in the activities of the world of everyday mortality with a strategy, refined and strengthened on the magic mountain, of dynamically serene and wise detachment.

Chapter 3

James Hilton

In this essay I will examine the quest of Hugh Conway, the protagonist of Hilton's *Lost Horizon* (1933), to achieve an expansive sense of space and time in a "magic mountain" environment. He seems destined to develop and fulfill this quest in the ambience of Shangri-La, a world beyond the constraints of mortality, representing a relatively timeless space pervaded by a quietly dynamic sense of aesthetic and intellectual serenity and vitality.

I will show that Hilton's protagonist affirms a Bergsonian life-philosophy in his quest for a sense of continuity with the world of Shangri-La. One essential aspect of Bergson's thought for Conway is the emphasis on duration as a free creation which is stressed by G. Poulet, for example, in his statement:

> There is no longer any opposition between moment and duration; no longer any trace of deterministic fatalism; but in place of the hiatus between the actual feeling of existence and the profundity of existence, there is the possibility of a mutual communication, of a relationship between the moment and time; and in place of a determinism of cause and effect, the feeling that any moment can be realized as a new moment, and that time can always be freely created from the present moment forward. (35)

Conway epitomizes in his character and life-strategy the diffusion of the opposition between moment and duration as well as the feeling that any moment can be realized as a new moment.

The first chapter of the novel describes the adventure from Baskul of Conway and his companions, kidnapped by an unknown pilot and taken unawares into the misty depths of mountainous silences. The trial and uncertainty of the journey are overcome, for Conway at least, by the sight of the mountain lamasery and the lushgreen, "delightfully favored" (82) valley below. The description of the journey reveals

Conway's tranquil courage and resolute serenity in difficult circum-
stances and affirms that he is a "delightfully favored" character destined to participate in vital events.

The first sight of the lamasery of Shangri-La is a dazzling, yet serene, vision of a timeless world, a timeless universe of dynamically
subtle thought and refined feeling. For Conway the initial perception
of the lamasery might have been a vision deriving from his sense of
physical tranquillity and harmony which he feels during the climb. The
description of the first view of Shangri-La is memorable not only for
its etherial quality, but also because it initiates Conway into the timeless world:

> It was, indeed, a strange and half-incredible sight. A group of colored pavil-
> ions clung to the mountainside with none of the grim deliberation of a
> Rhineland castle, but rather with the chance delicacy of flowerpetals impaled
> upon a crag. It was superb and exquisite. An austere emotion carried the eye
> upward from milk-blue roofs to the gray rock bastion above, tremendous as
> the Wetterhorn above Grindelwald. Beyond that, in a dazzling pyramid, soared
> the snow slopes of Karakal. (81)

The otherworldliness of the Tibetan ambience is reinforced by the
sense that the air, "clean as from another planet, was more precious
with every intake" (74). The conscious and deliberate breathing which
resulted inevitably in such an atmosphere produced ultimately "an almost ecstatic tranquillity of mind" (74) and "a single rhythm of breathing, walking and thinking" (74). Conway's serene personality achieves
an emotional unity with the aura of Shangri-La. He is instinctively a
spiritual disciple of the etherial timelessness of the lamasery world. In
sight of Karakal Conway willingly accepts this journey to Shangri-La
not as a dangerous challenge, but as a mind-opening and sense-ex-
panding opportunity, an exceptional occasion to develop his emotional, intellectual, and spiritual awareness.

Conway is instinctively destined to participate in a quest for timelessness at Shangri-La because he has the appropriate character and
life-philosophy to appreciate its profound serenity and timeless ambience. Conway's personality reveals a resilient balance of inner energy
and dynamic spectatorship. Hilton elaborates on this quality in Conway
to participate with an intuitive perceptiveness in life by saying that his
seeming indecisiveness at the approach of the strangers after the journey by plane was not bravery or self-confidence but "a form of indo-
lence, an unwillingness to interrupt his mere spectator's interest in
what was happening" (69). This passivity might be linked for Conway,

as it is for Castorp in Mann's *The Magic Mountain*, to the fact that neither protagonist creates the aura of timelessness in which he participates. Each is brought to it, initiated into it as a "passive" recipient of the timeless charm of the magic mountain atmosphere.

Although Conway is, or appears to be, fated to experience the timeless ambience of Shangri-La, the concrete development of his quest, unlike Castorp's journey to the Davos sanatorium in Mann's *The Magic Mountain*, is initiated by accident, by a seeming quirk of chance. Yet, this is perhaps what destiny is. For Castorp planned to go to the mountain sanatorium for a short visit whereas Conway did not plan, at least consciously, to be taken to a Tibetan monastery. Nevertheless, Conway, even before his arrival, is destined, in his learning process, to be the intellectual-aesthetic equal and heir of Father Perrault, whereas Castorp begins his stay at Davos as a student of Settembrini's and only gradually develops and asserts his intellectual vitality.

The seeming impregnability by foreign, unguided elements reinforces the otherworldly, timeless quality of this environment. Yet, from the beginning of the description of Shangri-La, it is clear (the manuscript's narrator wishes, perhaps less consciously than unconsciously, to make clear to us) that the feeling of permanence and timelessness is qualified by a realization that a natural catastrophe might, at an unexpected moment in the future, undermine this seemingly eternal world. After thinking that this spot represented the most terrifying mountainscape in the world, Conway imagines that the great strain of snow and glacier against which the rock served as a retaining wall might someday cause the mountain to split, sending deadly avalanches into the valley below. Moreover, the narrator is aware that the existing cleft below the mountain wall is a likely consequence of a past natural upheaval. This seeming fragility merely enhances the distinctive, etherial beauty of the Shangri-La ambience.

One might argue that Shangri-La is an exemplary aesthetic embodiment of E. M. Forster's internally harmonious work of art. Forster declares in *Two Cheers for Democracy* that a work of art is unique "not because it is clever or noble or beautiful or enlightened or original or sincere or idealistic or useful or educational—it may embody any of those qualities—but because it is the only material object in the universe which may possess internal harmony" (90). Shangri-La reveals the internal stability and harmonious order which are essential to the eternally significant and humanistically vital work of art. Moreover, Conway is the "artist" who has the aesthetic sensibility and emotional-intellectual sensitivity to appreciate Shangri-La's internal harmony.

The dream-like aura of Shangri-La gives Conway a vital sense of tranquillity. This sense of serenity is complemented by Conway's initial impression of the interior of the lamasery as being spacious, warm, and clean. He feels that he has entered a new world of elegant serenity and etherial beauty. The aura of Shangri-La represents in the aesthetic and intellectual tradition of Andre Malraux's *The Voices of Silence* a purification of the world and a serenely Promethean revolt against the temporal flux and vicissitudes of mortality.

At the beginning of chapter four there is a description of the life-philosophy which pervades Shangri-La and which Conway has cultivated instinctively in his own life: "He was enjoying that pleasant mingling of physical ease and mental alertness which seemed to him, of all sensations, the most truly civilized" (85). Shangri-La does possess the material accoutrements of a civilized Western society such as central heating. Perhaps most importantly for its self-defined and self-determined mission of cultural-intellectual preservation Shangri-La fuses features of Western and Eastern civilization (for example, significant literary texts of both traditions).

It is important, especially in light of the task which Perrault will give to Conway, that Conway feels at home in the lamasery ambience. By feeling emotionally and spiritually at one with this ambience, and by preserving that sense of unity, Conway enables himself to fulfill his quest for timelessness. Not only does he share the life-philosophy of Shangri-La (with its devotion to a contemplative appreciation of wisdom and culture) intimately, but his first meal, which was Chinese, gave him a sense of familiarity here, for he had spent several congenial years in China. This sudden acclimatization on the part of Conway contrasts sharply with the early experience of Hans Castorp who does not initially feel at home on his magic mountain. Perhaps one might argue that Hans Castorp starts his magic mountain experience as a Mallinson-type, but ultimately develops into a Conway-like character with intellectual self-confidence and emotional-psychological assurance. Yet, Castorp's final significant action of departure from the Berghof may, in its ambivalence of motivation and outcome, be a gesture of Mallinson- or Conway-like vitality.

Both Conway and Castorp seem fated to have come to their respective magic mountains. Conway's past almost appears as a consciously designed preparation for the physical, intellectual, and spiritual challenges of Shangri-La. Castorp showed from early childhood a subtle appreciation of death—moreover, he is described as being a good patient, an individual suited to participate in the Berghof experience.

Conway's feeling of comfort after he has been at Shangri-La for a short while is stressed several times. While Conway finds the atmosphere of the lamasery agreeable, he wonders how the others are adapting and surviving, for he senses that his companions do not share his enthusiasm for this unique context. This outward-directed concern of Conway is important because it suggests that he is capable, at least potentially, of fulfilling the role which the leader of the lamasery will offer to him.

Conway's quest for timelessness is simultaneously a quest for aesthetic enrichment. Conway's experience of Shangri-La will not only develop his sense of time and potential timelessness—it will also enhance his aesthetic awareness. Perhaps these two features are inextricably linked. The aesthetic education of Conway is strengthened in his perception of treasures that museums and millionaires alike would be interested in. These treasures include pearl blue Sung ceramics, paintings in tinted inks, and beautiful lacquers.

The exquisitely fragile beauty of the artistic objects is reinforced in the following description of the Shangri-La aura: "A world of incomparable refinements still lingered tremulously in porcelain and varnish, yielding an instant of emotion before its dissolution into purest thought" (114). The dissolution of the instant of emotion into purest thought transforms the vitality of the aesthetic image (in Pound's sense of the image as an emotional and intellectual complex in an instant of time) into an aura of artistically etherial contemplation. By appreciating the delicate beauty of such art objects, Conway participates aesthetically and emotionally in the world of Shangri-La.

Conway's aesthetic vitality is refined in the scene where he takes a stroll after dinner and comes to the terrace leaning over the valley. He is described as being embraced by the scent of tuberose (called in China the smell of moonlight) and thinking that if the moonlight had a sound also it might be the Rameau gavotte which Lo-Tsen had recently played.

Conway's sense of being at home is enhanced by his congenial response to the material qualities of the room—the fact that it is well proportioned and tastefully adorned with tapestries and pieces of lacquer. The sense of comfort, Conway assumes, has been strengthened by the use of a drug in their food—and yet, Conway is not apprehensive because such a substance has had a salutary effect not only on himself but also on Barnard and Mallinson. Conway's experience of a soothing comfort of mind and body is reinforced by the timeless ambience of Shangri-La. For example, the image of the paper lanterns, motionless in the still air, articulates subtly the pervasively serene permanence and timelessness of Shangri-La.

In conversation with Conway and Miss Brinklow, Chang describes the life-philosophy of the lamasery as a devotion to the notion of moderation, involving the avoidance of excess and tempestuousness. Chang notices the calm and patience of Conway in responding to his new surroundings and expresses his conviction in and gratefulness for the wisdom of this British consular officer.

Although he is not eager to depart, Conway assumes the role of information-gatherer for his fellow travellers and asks Chang about hiring porters. In the ensuing discussion Conway expresses his feeling that the meeting with Chang and his porters near the crash of the plane carrying Conway and his companions was not fortuitous. Chang's response affirms Conway's intuition that their arrival was expected. This is important because it suggests that at least one member of the party taken from Baskul, most likely Conway, was chosen and destined to come to Shangri-La.

The timeless ambience of Shangri-La is enhanced by the presence of "the gleaming pyramid of Karakal" (97), which has a seemingly mesmerizing effect on Conway, infusing him with a profound sense of repose. Conway envisions Karakal, meaning Blue Moon, as a lighthouse brooding serenely over the valley beyond time.

One might compare the sense of timelessness in Shangri-La to the theme of the transcendence of time at the end of Fitzgerald's *The Great Gatsby*. Fitzgerald speaks of a transitory enchanted moment referring to the contemplative wonder of the early settlers in the New World. Nick Carraway is contemplating the ocean and imagines in the moonlight darkness the natural ambience and emotional-spiritual reaction of early Dutch settlers in the New World:

> Its vanished trees, the trees that had made way for Gatsby's house, had once pandered in whispers to the last and greatest of all human dreams; for a transitory enchanted moment man must have held his breath in the presence of this continent, compelled into an aesthetic contemplation he neither understood nor desired, face to face for the last time in history with something commensurate to his capacity for wonder. (182)

Carraway reflects in this transitory enchanted moment upon another new world as well—the world of extravagance, leisure, and opulence which Gatsby created and tries to sustain. Such a contemplative activity, which includes the consideration of Gatsby's romance with Daisy and the inherently corrupt world of Tom and Daisy, is one which Nick does not necessarily understand or desire. The transitory enchanted moment is preserved and enhanced only because of Nick's admiration for the mythical Gatsby.

Conway appears to experience a similar enchanted moment, though perhaps less transitory, of aesthetic appreciation in contemplating Shangri-La initially. Although Conway is "compelled" into the aesthetic contemplation of Shangri-La, it is a contemplation he understands and desires intuitively and sincerely. Conway's experience of the enchanted moment of Shangri-La is more affirmational and affirmative than Nick's "transitory enchanted moment." Conway's adventure in Shangri-La might be described as a series of enchanted moments which transcend any possible transitoriness, culminating in the supreme enchanted moment of his congenially etherial encounter with the High Lama. Like the perfected mind in Shelley's *Prometheus Unbound* that achieves a sense of illimitable time, so Conway, through his Shangri-La experience, signifies a perpetual timelessness, an eternally sustained moment of timelessness, of timeless expansiveness, of the inner self.

Conway's difference from his Western companions is marked even at the early stage of the narrative, for he is somewhat exhilarated by the climb towards the lamasery while Mallinson, Barnard, and Miss Brinklow are struggling physically. This distinction is preserved throughout the course of the novel as Conway is presented consistently as a unique personality with the capacity to guide the world of Shangri-La.

Conway's differentiation from his fellow-travelers, signified not only by his greater familiarity with this part of the world but also by his leadership potential is further dramatized when he shows his knowledge of rope-craft. The fact that Conway had once been a first-class mountaineer reinforces the inevitability of his position of authority. In response to Mallinson's worried concerns about their immediate future, Conway says that there are times in life when the most appropriate reaction is to do nothing at all or to approach problematic situations, such as the war, with a passively vital wisdom.

Mallinson wonders how Conway can seem so emotionally cool and collected at such a difficult moment. Conway responds that is because he can recall so many other things which seemed nightmarish as well. One wonders whether Conway has become or has compelled himself to become hardened to such nightmarish events, or whether he still suffers emotionally under the strain of such novel experiences. Or perhaps we should accept Conway's own statement that he has developed a rather cynical approach to life, exemplified in his comment to Mallinson that in undertaking this excursion to the unknown they have merely exchanged one form of lunacy for another.

Hugh Conway reflects to himself upon his official capacity—the official part of Conway believes that, as a representative of the British government, his requests for information should be cordially answered. In the same spirit Conway reflects on his leadership capacity—he muses that he should be given an award for his protection of scores of civilians in a small consulate during a revolution. Yet he knows that he is not an empire-building leader. For the most salient, the most vital dimension of his character is not his official, but his personal capacity of emotional-spiritual awareness and openness to new ideas and experiences.

Shangri-La gradually exerts an increasingly more enchanting influence over its newest devotee. When Conway rose the next morning, he would not have wished to be anywhere else in the world. However, one might claim that it is not merely Shangri-La itself, but the "puzzle of Shangri-La" (100) which fascinates Conway.

In chapter five we learn of Conway's burgeoning enchantment with Shangri-La and its ambience: "It was not so much any individual thing that attracted him as the gradual revelation of elegance, of modest and impeccable taste, of harmony so fragrant that it seemed to gratify the eye without arresting it" (113). The tour of Shangri-La enhances Conway's enchantment considerably. The artistic treasures of the lamasery reveal "an air of having fluttered into existence like petals from a flower" (114).

The description of the library reinforces the serenely wise tone of the lamasery. The library is a sanctuary characterized by and infused with an ambience of lofty spaciousness as well as of good manners and profound wisdom. The library offers a balance of the world's best literature in addition to a variety of more abstruse material. As in the material, physical qualities of the lamasery, the Shangri-La library represents a harmonious balance of Western and Eastern texts. Conway, because of his capacity for seriousness and studiousness in private and public activity, feels very much at home emotionally, intellectually, and spiritually in this environment.

However, Conway, despite the emotional-spiritual happiness which he develops and sustains here relatively easily, remains periodically puzzled. He wonders not only why he seemed to have been chosen for Shangri-La but also about the implausible existence of this extraordinarily unique cultural oasis in the middle of a forbidding winter wilderness. These concerns and doubts are softened by the congenially austere serenity of Shangri-La and by Conway's intuition that the etherial timelessness of the lamasery will resolve his questionings.

In chapter six Conway feels that he is becoming gradually able to understand Chang better, especially with respect to his philosophy of time. Conway says to Chang that in the world of Shangri-La time, the flux of time, is much less significant than it is to the world of everyday mortality beyond Shangri-La. Conway proceeds to say that if he were in London he would not be eager to see the latest hour-old newspaper—likewise, the people at Shangri-La are no more interested in seeing a year-old one. Such a passage affirms Conway's potential to liberate himself emotionally and spiritually from the flux of mortality.

In chapter seven we learn about the history of Shangri-La in the conversation between Conway and the High Lama. The remarkable story which the High Lama tells is his own story: the story of the Capuchin friar who, near death on his search for traces of the Nestorian faith, accidentally came upon the only approach to the valley of the Blue Moon. In 1734, at the age of fifty-three, the friar started to repair and transform the buildings of an ancient lamasery into a Christian monastery.

The friar's name was Perrault. He was a worldly scholar who wanted to teach his converts the importance of an intellectual-spiritual-physical balance in their lives. The High Lama describes Perrault as an earnest, busy, learned, simple, and enthusiastic person who could function effectively as a priest or as a mason helping to build the monastery rooms. The High Lama speaks of Perrault's advancing, yet still productive, years and of the clarity of mind which he gradually attained. When he was 108 years of age, Perrault seemed to be on the verge of dying; however, he managed, perhaps miraculously, to recover.

Perrault achieved a legendary significance and was believed to be able to work miracles in his quasi-divine status. The High Lama describes Perrault's attitude as one of quiet perseverance—because he did not die at a normal age he felt that he could seemingly live forever. Perrault preserved the tranquil tastes of a scholar. To keep himself intellectually occupied Perrault translated Montaigne's essay on vanity into Tibetan.

In 1804 another European stranger arrived in the valley of the Blue Moon. This stranger, named Henschell, was initially interested in the gold deposits of the valley but gradually came to be enchanted by the atmosphere of etherial tranquillity and rarefied freedom. He was the one who began the lamasery collections of Chinese art and the library and musical acquisitions. Henschell suggested that strangers be welcomed at Shangri-La. He was unfortunately killed in a dispute at Shangri-La.

By the end of the High Lama's narrative Conway realizes that Father Perrault is none other than the High Lama himself. Father Perrault, the High Lama, goes on to say that his favorite Western composer is Mozart because his music reveals "an austere elegance" (180). The phrase "austere elegance" is important not only as an interpretation of the music of Mozart, but also because it captures the spirit of the lamasery. Shangri-La exemplifies to a considerable extent the life-philosophy which strives, consciously and unconsciously, to attain an austere elegance, a noble simplicity and quiet grandeur. There is a distinctively Mozartian undertone to the lamasery's quest for moderation.

Father Perrault proceeds to explain to Conway why he and his companions were chosen and why they will remain in Shangri-La "for good" (180). He also offers some interesting reflections on life and time which correspond closely to Conway's philosophy of life and time. Perrault tells Conway that by the standards of Shangri-La his sunlit years have scarcely begun. He suggests to Conway that he may preserve a long and wondrous youth, that at eighty he may climb to the pass with a young man's gait. Despite the sense of seeming immortality which Perrault conveys, he concludes this thought with a sobering return to a stridently realistic awareness of transitoriness. Though Shangri-La can diminish the tempo of life and postpone mortality, Perrault admits that no conquest of death or decay has been made.

Perrault then makes the most convincing and effective argument of the entire work about the advantages of staying at Shangri-La. In the passage of time at Shangri-La one will move from physical pleasures into more austere and no less satisfying realms of enjoyment where one may achieve serenity, profundity, and wisdom. And most important of all, one will have an abundance, an exuberance of time.

What is so important about Perrault's statement is not only that he captures the philosophical and spiritual essence of Shangri-La so powerfully, but also that he expresses himself in a softly transcendent tone which reinforces and strengthens his message. Perrault continues to address his kindred spirit, Conway, in a timelessly gentle tone saying that he will have time to read and enjoy music, among other activities, in an aura of "unruffled and unmeasured" (186) Time.

If there is a sense of religion here, it is perhaps this conception of time linked with the awareness of the importance of cultural preservation as opposed to any specific orthodoxy. In contrast to the strictly Christian atmosphere of the monastery of the Grande Chartreuse, Shangri-La offers an environment which is less religious than spiritual in its Buddhist and Christian connections. In Wordsworth, by contrast, one might say that the sense of religion derives from the belief in the presence of the divine in the spatial and temporal expansiveness of nature. Wordsworth's Mt. Snowdon is a place of pantheistic dynamism of orphic proportions, whereas Arnold's Grande Chartreuse is a more hermetically soothing space. Hilton's Shangri-La, aspiring to preserve the ecumenically powerful spirit of the Mt. Snowdon vision, represents a relatively timeless present of orphic and hermetic vitality.

Perhaps because Conway has expressed some doubt as to the possibility of spending the rest of his life in this mountain lamasery-retreat (though his doubt seems to be expressed more for the sake of his friends than for himself) Perrault maintains that whether Conway seeks intellectual and emotional fellowship with others or the splendid isolation of his own thoughts he can find a most congenial ambience at Shangri-La.

Conway responds that he does find a charm and quietude at the lamasery which appeals to him—he says that he has expended much energy and passion already and that now he is only interested in being left alone by the world. Perrault senses the exceptional uniqueness of Conway's emotional, intellectual, and spiritual character and expresses his admiration for Conway's clarity of mind. For both individuals, the notion of "clarity of mind" is symbolic of, if not synonymous with, wisdom. Conway, having experienced, especially during the First World War, the heat, passions, and chaos of mortal existence, has gradually become a sensitive philosopher of life, of the contemplative life devoted to beauty and wisdom—such a life-strategy projects him perfectly into the role of successor to Father Perrault.

Conway might be said to signify R.W. Emerson's "scholar"-figure. This capacity for serene wisdom is one of the primary qualities which the High Lama sees in Conway which encourages him to believe in Conway's potential to assume a leadership role in Shangri-La. Conway has what Emerson calls in his address "The American Scholar" a heroic mind and an active soul. In the mission to preserve the cultural and intellectual heritage of humankind the High Lama reveals himself as the Emersonian "scholar" who appreciates and understands the universal truths beyond appearance.

In concluding his address Emerson writes: "The scholar is that man who must take up into himself all the ability of the time, all the contributions of the past, all the hopes of the future. He must be a university of knowledge" (113). Emerson's scholar represents universal mind, universal soul, universal humanity—he is an exemplary individual of mythological vitality. Such individuals are the High Lama and Hugh Conway, although Conway, because of an externally motivated inner tension, is more at pains to conceal his potential to signify such mythological vitality.

In response to Conway's wondering about the purpose of life, the High Lama asserts that Shangri-La has a definite and important function. Shangri-La exists to preserve the cultural and intellectual legacy of the world and to preserve a vision of hope in a world which has the potential and often seemingly the penchant to destroy itself. The High Lama cherishes the hope, as strong as it is fragile, that Shangri-La will overcome any doomsday cataclysm which may destroy the world. He hopes that Shangri-La, as a sanctuary with such an important cultural heritage to bequeath, will be ignored by the tempestuousness and violence of the world.

Perrault sees the mission of Shangri-La not only as a vital activity of cultural and intellectual importance, but also as a means of fulfilling the ethic that the meek shall inherit the earth. One might say that Perrault, the High Lama, is an embodiment of the philosopher-king as described in Plato's "Programme of Studies." Not only has he preserved his intellectual and physical health and developed his capacity to see the connections of things but he believes that the search for truth and the continual revitalization of that search are of the utmost importance. The High Lama of Shangri-La reveals a sense of justice which transcends the normative legal parameters of the world into the realm of justice which is defined by eternally significant aesthetic, intellectual, and spiritual concerns.

The conversation between the High Lama and Conway ends as it began—in an atmosphere of quiet, etherial serenity. For Conway this is a blissfully profound serenity: "Never had Shangri-La offered more concentrated loveliness to his eyes; the valley lay imaged over the edge of the cliff, and the image was of a deep unrippled pool that matched the peace of his own thoughts" (192).

Conway speaks somewhat later of his need for equanimity to achieve a balance in his life between his desire to be honest with his fellow passengers from Baskul and the necessity of keeping silent about his knowledge of their participation in the present and future mission of Shangri-La. Like Hans Castorp in Thomas Mann's *The Magic Mountain*, Conway feels time expanding and space contracting. Unlike Castorp, however, Conway experiences a tension between his two lives, between the life which, perhaps more reinforced by the sentiments of Mallinson than he is willing to admit, yearns, not intensely but gently, for escape from Shangri-La at some indefinite moment in the future, and the life which realizes that Shangri-La is an ideal place to be fully admired, appreciated, and respected.

In wondering which of his two lives is more real Conway reflects upon severe bombardments in the war during which he had the sensation that he possessed many lives, only one of which could be taken by death. This passage is extremely important not only because it stresses Conway's conviction in the multiple potentialities of his Self, but also because it shows Conway's concern for transcending mortality. One might even consider such war-time meditations as a foreshadowing of Conway's inevitable arrival at Shangri-La. For the foundation of Conway's intellectual clarity and emotional-spiritual wisdom had been established even then.

The metaphysical tension engendered by the existence of two lives, the presence of two strategies of the self, is articulated well by Reinhold Niebuhr in *The Self and the Dramas of History*:

> It is obvious that the self's freedom over natural process enables it to be a creator of historical events. Both its memory of past events and its capacity to project goals transcending the necessities of nature enable it to create the new level of reality which we know as human history. But the self is not simply a creator of his new dimension, for it is also a creature of the web of events, in the creation of which it participates. (158)

Conway embodies this metaphysical tension, creating and being created by events, ultimately asserting the freedom of the self over natural process by aspiring to become an integral part of Shangri-La.

Conway finally hears Chang's story as well. In revealing his personal tale, Chang emphasizes the importance of the atmosphere of the valley of the Blue Moon. Chang, now 97, having arrived in Shangri-La at age 22, says that if he had left the valley years ago he certainly would have been dead already. To reinforce his point about the significantly more rapid aging process outside of Shangri-La and the valley of the Blue Moon, Chang gives the example of a man who arrived at Shangri-La in the prime of his life and who, when he reached eighty, looked only half that old. He left the valley to look for an approaching party, but was captured by nomads and kept away for much longer than a week (the interval of a week would not have made a crucial difference). When he returned this man showed his real age in his face and in his behavior and soon died, as an old man.

After reflecting for a while, Conway reacts by describing time as a monstrous force lurking outside the valley to attack the "slackers" who have evaded him. Chang, after Conway has explained the unfamiliar colloquialism, says that Shangri-La does not consider slackness a vice—rather the people of Shangri-La prefer slackness greatly to tension, which dominates the outside world. Conway, who did not initially use the word in a negative tone, ends the exchange by saying that he is inclined to agree with Chang. Perhaps one should say that, while not using the word "slacker" to apply negatively to any of the Shangri-La inhabitants, Conway uses it, perhaps somewhat unconsciously, to apply to himself. One might argue that he sees himself (or rather, a part of his Self) as a slacker, and is refreshed to hear Chang's positive interpretation of the term.

The patient flux of time at Shangri-La, which gives the semblance of timeless fluidity, is reinforced by Conway's sensation of the profoundly serene atmosphere in which urgency does not clamor nor postponement disappoint. This sensation develops in the context of Chang's statement that Conway may not meet some of the lamas for quite a while.

Conway does eventually meet several lamas, the distinguishing, shared qualities of whom are an agelessness and a calm intelligence characterized by measured and well-balanced opinions. It is not surprising that Conway gets along well with the lamas, for his intellect and temperament are so perfectly suited to Shangri-La and to their company.

Conway notices that the lamas with whom he talked have a powerful capacity to recollect their pre-Tibetan lives. Chang asserts that the development of such a capability belongs to the training of the lamas which involves the clarifying of the mind so as to obtain a panorama of one's past in viable perspective. Chang proceeds to say that in this process of refining one's perception of the past everything will emerge as clear and duly proportioned and with its proper significance.

The individual who has achieved a sense of aesthetic, emotional, intellectual, and spiritual unity with Shangri-La and with the Shangri-La ambience will experience an appreciation and understanding of the temporal continuum, the dynamic continuum of time, which is defined most effectively perhaps by the reciprocally vital interrelatedness of past, present, and future. The recollection, the creative revitalization of significant, seminal events in one's past gives one a sense of a perpetual present, a present intimately connected with and actively participating in the past and the future.

For Conway, however, the present is of the utmost personal importance. In various activities, whether reading in the library, or playing Mozart in the music room, Conway felt "a deep spiritual emotion, as if Shangri-La were indeed a living essence, distilled from the magic of the ages and miraculously preserved against time and death" (205). The image of Shangri-La as a distilled essence reinforces the semblance of alchemistic uniqueness which characterizes and emanates from Shangri-La.

The aura of Shangri-La is influenced by and similar to the aura of some American luminist painting of the nineteenth century. What Barbara Novak says in her essay "On Defining Luminism" about the qualities of American luminist painting may offer some interesting insights into and parallels to the light, silence, and atmosphere of Hilton's Shangri-La. Novak, in describing luminist light as "cool, not hot, hard, not soft, palpable rather than fluid, planar rather than atmospherically diffuse" (25), speaks also of its smooth glow. Novak writes of luminist silence that it implies presence through the sense of thereness rather than through action. She proceeds to conclude that in the repose of inaction luminist silence "represents not a void but a palpable space, in which everything happens while nothing does. We have here a visual analogue of Eckhart's 'central silence' and Thoreau's 'restful kernel in the magazine of the universe'" (28).

The aura of Hilton's Shangri-La is extraordinarily similar to that of American luminist paintings by M. J. Heade, Fitz Hugh Lane, and J. F. Kensett. The ambience of Shangri-La fuses the hermetically vital space of J. F. Kensett's *The White Mountains—Mt. Washington* (1851) and the etherial tranquillity of Fitz Hugh Lane's *Brace's Rock, Brace's Cove* (1864) and M. J. Heade's *Sunrise on the Marshes* (1863). Heade's *Lake George* (1862) offers a poignantly similar thematic focus to that of Hilton's Shangri-La. As Heade stresses the presence of a sublime space that complements the striving of the persona for infinity, so Hilton offers the narrative of an individual who through the dynamically hermetic space of Shangri-La envisions a diastolic time.

The timeless aura of Shangri-La is intimately related to the timeless aura of the space portrayed in Kensett's *The White Mountains—Mt. Washington*. Kensett's painting captures the etherial tranquillity of a space seemingly isolated from the ravages of everyday mortality and the negative consequences of industrial-material progress. Although not as secluded and sheltered as Shangri-La, the space of Kensett's painting represents a world which fulfills at least some of Shangri-La's promise of timeless enchantment.

Shangri-La not only offers Conway a new existential context in which to refine his wisdom—it also provides him with an opportunity to enrich and expand his knowledge in various intellectual domains. For example, he talks to Briac, a former student of Chopin, about Chopin and even memorizes several Chopin compositions which had never been published. This experience is important symbolically as well because it suggests, if not strengthens, the otherworldliness of Shangri-La by showing that Conway has access to knowledge and wisdom beyond the normal conceptual and perceptual limits of everyday mortality and reality.

When Conway asks Chang how soon he believes that the High Lama will call for him again, Chang projects that it will be at the end of the first five years of his sojourn at Shangri-La. However, less than a month after his arrival at the lamasery Conway receives a second invitation to see the leading figure in this seemingly timeless world.

The extraordinariness of this second visit vanishes when Conway is invited to see the High Lama a third and a fourth time. Hilton describes the supremely congenial meeting between these two kindred spirits, as aesthetically and intellectually close to one another as Thomas Cole and William Cullen Bryant in Asher Durand's painting *Kindred Spirits* (1849), as distinguished by a sumptuous tranquillity. The timeless aura of Shangri-La is strengthened and heightened by the all-embracing, all-encompassing nature of the tranquillity. But this is not a passive tranquillity—it is an active tranquillity which participates gently and quietly in the benevolent wisdom which it reinforces.

The profoundly etherial serenity allows and inspires Conway and the High Lama to reevaluate and reexamine entire philosophies and historical spans. Both are emotionally, intellectually, and spiritually enriched, if not symbolically transformed, by the vital exchange. The High Lama, sufficiently impressed by Conway to remark that his wisdom has the ripeness of age, exclaims that he has never met anyone like Conway before. Conway, in stating that he has lived more intensely than others earlier in his life, says that perhaps the exhaustion of the passions is the beginning of wisdom. When the High Lama affirms that such a view represents the essential doctrine of Shangri-La (although expressed in a different way), Conway says that he has already realized the significance of this doctrine in the Shangri-La life-philosophy and that he feels thoroughly at home in such a humanistically vital aura.

Conway is enraptured by Karakal and Shangri-La, from the vision of the gleaming, pure, elusive mountains to the perception of the silvery tones of the harpsichord floating across the lotus-pool. In this aura of enchantment Conway, like the protagonist in H.G. Wells' *The Time Machine*, feels that he has time for everything. This is what timelessness means to a mortal being, perhaps this is the only timelessness that a mortal can aspire to and even achieve—the emotional and intellectual sensation of having all the time in the world. Conway has time for everything that he wished to happen, so much time that desire itself was satisfied in the certainty of fulfillment. The individual who is emotionally and spiritually attuned to the lamasery world and to its vision and presence of timelessness becomes an integral dimension of its nonlinear, suspended inner "time."

The vast majority of mortal beings live and fulfill their lives at odds with and in conflict with time. Time is an external force, an externally alien phenomenon, to be disdained and feared as much as it is to be competed against. For the individual who has developed a Shangri-La philosophy of life, time is no longer an inimical antagonist. Rather, such an individual internalizes time, he suspends the temporal flux of his own life in his own self-determined, self-generated conception of time. There exists a complementary relation between such an individual and time. Such an individual, whose life becomes, either consciously or unconsciously, a quest to transcend mortality, fulfills the challenge and promise of Whitman's persona in "Song of Myself" who laughs at dissolution (the dissolution of the self through mortality) and asserts that he knows the amplitude of time.

Conway, like Mallinson, is attracted to and intrigued by Lo-Tsen. Unlike Claudia Chauchat in Mann's *The Magic Mountain*, Lo-Tsen gives primarily emotional-spiritual comfort, sparing her lovers moments of satiety. Lo-Tsen epitomizes the strategy of moderation which pervades the timeless aura of Shangri-La. In contrasting Lo-Tsen with Cleopatra, Chang says that Lo-Tsen removes hunger where she least satisfies. He says that she, like Shangri-La itself, has an exceptionally subtle capability of calming desire to a murmur which is no less pleasant when left unanswered.

Affected strongly by both Shangri-La and Lo-Tsen, Conway muses that he has never been so happy, even during his life before the war. He is emotionally and intellectually captivated and aesthetically entranced by the divinely serene aura of Shangri-La where "feelings were sheathed in thoughts, and thoughts softened into felicity by their transference into language" (227).

Conway appreciates the congenially leisurely atmosphere in which conversation represents and reveals emotional and intellectual accomplishment, not merely habit. The outward tranquillity of Shangri-La conceals and reinforces the active intellectual lives of the lamas, many of whom were devoted to writing books. The quietly dynamic pursuits of the lamas, which may have seemed secondary or unusual to the external world of everyday mortality, complement the intellectually and spiritually ecumenical atmosphere of Shangri-La.

The importance of perspective is discussed briefly in the novel— this is a discussion at the core of the perception of Shangri-La. The High Lama, who now converses often and freely with Conway, says to him that the people of the valley of the Blue Moon use the word "outside" to refer not only to the environment beyond the pass but also to the entire world beyond Shangri-La. They live in a centripetal, self-directed world which is congenially self-contained—they do not believe that anyone would ever wish to leave their beautiful valley. Moreover, they believe that all "outsiders" who appear at the pass greatly desire, whether or not they wish to admit it consciously, to enter their world.

In the ensuing discussion the High Lama tells Conway that he feels he is dying, and he chooses Conway as his successor to preserve and strengthen the heritage and mission of Shangri-La. The High Lama, in saying that he has waited for Conway for a long time, senses that Conway has an awareness, maturity, and wisdom far beyond his years. The High Lama proceeds to affirm to Conway the essential goals of Shangri-La: to nurture and to preserve a spirit of gentleness, patience, and wisdom, and to develop and to sustain a cultural and an intellectual vitality. He concludes by asserting that it will be easy for Conway to assume the leadership of Shangri-La and he is certain that Conway will find great happiness in such a position.

Hugh Conway, as Father Perrault consciously and intuitively knew and knows, is a burgeoning philosopher-king, a developing Emersonian "scholar" who is as vital as the profoundly vital creative individual described in William Faulkner's Nobel Prize address. Conway is John Stuart Mill's eccentric and energetic character who understands the importance of cultural and intellectual cultivation and emotional and spiritual self-development and who is not merely knowledgeable of human culture and nature, but most importantly humanistically insightful and compassionately wise.

As he returns to his living quarters after the final discussion with the High Lama, Conway is jolted out of his musing by Mallinson, who exclaims that the porters have arrived. Conway and Mallinson have a lengthy discussion in which Mallinson represents the typical skeptic who does not and will not appreciate and understand the beauty and significance of Shangri-La. Mallinson tries to persuade Conway to join him and Lo-Tsen in leaving. Ultimately and surprisingly, Conway decides to depart with Mallinson. The reason for Conway's decision is not clear—it is as spontaneous as the appearance of Shangri-La itself in the wintry mists of a mountain wilderness.

Does Conway leave to help Mallinson and Lo-Tsen because he senses they are in love? Is this the old Conway, the Baskul Conway, the self-sacrificial leader of individuals in trouble, who rises to the occasion? Does he leave because he senses that his affection for Lo-Tsen can only remain a broken dream because of her seeming attraction to Mallinson? In this situation is Conway not like Dexter Green of Fitzgerald's "Winter Dreams," who becomes aware of his own mortality and of the transience of the human condition when he hears that Judy, his "dream-woman," is no longer the radiantly dynamic and youthful spirit she used to be? Has Conway perhaps become so troubled in his own mind by Mallinson's doubting, questioning attitude that he has come to doubt the vitality of Shangri-La's etherial beauty and profound tranquillity? As Conway goes to the balcony to gaze at the dazzling plume of Karakal, it seems to him as if a dream had dissolved in the presence of harsh reality.

Does not Conway seem to fall into the trap, whether consciously or unconsciously set by Mallinson, which Mallinson accuses him of falling into with respect to the positive statements about Shangri-La made by the High Lama and Chang? Does Conway respond so easily and carelessly to Mallinson's critical insinuations and adamant doubts because he sees in Mallinson himself, a younger Self? Is this why he sacrifices a potentially glorious life at Shangri-La—not to save Mallinson in an official capacity, but to save him out of personal duty and inclination for a future life in his own chosen existential context, a chaotic world of stark everyday realities?

Perhaps Conway's mind is in such turmoil at this point because he feels a responsibility both to the High Lama and the mission of Shangri-La on the one hand and to Mallinson, the conspicuously suffering fellow countryman and younger Self, on the other. One might argue that Conway chooses in favor of Mallinson—and his decision to depart is a choice, as abrupt and erratic as it seems—because he feels that Shangri-La is so capable of preserving itself and that any of the lamas would be eminently qualified to guide this sanctuary into a productively serene future.

Mallinson, however, needs guidance to return to his former life. Yet, one cannot help wondering whether Conway really appreciated the decision which the High Lama made in choosing him to be his successor. Is Conway's decision to leave and abandon Shangri-La without his leadership not too careless for someone of such seemingly vital emotional and intellectual sensitivity? Or does Conway leave because he does not feel that he is suited to the task?

Does Conway depart because, like Castorp in Mann's *The Magic Mountain*, he is more bourgeois and democratically inclined than he wishes to admit consciously? Does Conway leave to escape his own genius, his own gradually refined capacity to symbolize the Nietzschean "Übermensch," the aesthetic innovator and intellectual iconoclast? John Stuart Mill writes in *On Liberty*:

> Genius can only breathe in an atmosphere of freedom. Persons of genius are, ex vi termini, more individual than any other people—less capable, consequently, of fitting themselves, without hurtful compression, into any of the small number of molds which society provides in order to save its members the trouble of forming their own character. (62)

Shangri-La certainly offers an atmosphere of freedom—yet, at the same time, one might wonder whether Conway feels somewhat pressured here to assume the kind of position of supreme responsibility which he has been assiduously and effectively avoiding in his career. Perhaps Conway exits suddenly to escape the possible tensions inherent in a dynamic leadership role. On the one hand, he does not want to experience excessive individuality and on the other hand, he wants to excuse himself from the "pressure" (a notion perhaps more imaginary and virtual than realistic and actual) of guiding Shangri-La and preserving and strengthening its sacred, universally significant mission.

Does Conway, a conscientious civil servant perhaps have the "burden" of Erasmus' *The Education of the Christian Prince* in mind when he abdicates his potential leadership role? Erasmus wrote in the tradition of Plato and Cicero that only the individual who has no desire to rule is fit to be a ruler. Being a ruler means bearing a cross—because the truly devoted ruler must assume widespread cares, forego pleasures, and work long hours to assure the security and happiness of his subjects. Conway could certainly have led Shangri-La with humane wisdom and gentle authority—perhaps he is "too fit" to rule or guide Shangri-La.

It is interesting that Charles, to whom *The Education of the Christian Prince* is addressed, would soon become Holy Roman Emperor—years later he would abdicate his throne and enter a monastery. Conway ultimately seems to deny or sublimate his capacity to guide this dynamically monastic environment and returns instead to the everyday world of temporally defined reality.

Conway leaves not only because he feels a personal commitment to Mallinson, but also because the dream-like aura of Shangri-La, heightened in his discussion with the High Lama, has been undermined, if not shattered, by Mallinson's critical realism. Yet, if Conway does view Mallinson as a younger version or vision of himself, or if he sees in Mallinson qualities which he showed at that age as well, why does he not try to persuade Mallinson to stay at Shangri-La to allow his inner wisdom to mature and ripen?

Even Rutherford, who records Conway's narrative, remarks on Conway's departure with subtle disbelief—he is surprised that Conway should have forsaken the blessed sanctuary in which he had found such happiness. Rutherford, however, does offer a provisional answer to the question of Conway's motivation to depart—this occurs when Conway is preparing the rope at the precipice, at the fragile edge of Shangri-La. Rutherford asserts not only that Conway is at heart a wanderer, but also that he feels instinctively a personal and a social obligation to help Mallinson, though such an endeavor challenges his own sense of wisdom. That Conway is at heart a wanderer is sug-

gested by the fact that he has lived in various places on multiple as-
signments. Yet there seems to be a metaphysical conflict here, because Conway himself admits that he is naturally rather lazy (which is
really a dynamic state of repose) and that he cherishes the timeless
serenity of Shangri-La.

After Mallinson has been helped over the precipice by Conway, he
says to Conway that it is wonderful to see that he is back to normal,
that his real self has once again emerged. However, one cannot help
asking whether the self which Mallinson perceives to be Conway's
"real self" is such at all. Might one not claim that Conway's real self,
his inner self which appreciates and cherishes serenity and wisdom,
still remains and will forever remain at Shangri-La? The self which
Mallinson observes is merely one of multiple external manifestations
(or kindred mutations) of the real self of Conway which will always
reside in the wise moderation of the profound tranquillity of Shangri-
La.

We are told by Rutherford that Conway not only survived the journey back to "civilization" from Shangri-La, but, once recovering from
his amnesia, he presumably tried to return to the oasis of transcendent quietude and truth in the Tibetan mountain wilderness. But does
Conway truly need to return to the tangible Shangri-La above the etherial valley of the Blue Moon? Does he not realize—and is this not one
of the reasons why he decides to leave Shangri-La—that Shangri-La is
most importantly a state of mind? Does Conway not realize in his
experience of the timeless serenity of Shangri-La and in his conversations with the High Lama that he has already experienced such timeless serenity before in his life?

One might argue that Conway realizes that he has already established a Shangri-La of the mind, reinforced by the vitality of his inner
wisdom. Moreover, Conway senses that he has an obligation, if not a
humanitarian privilege, not only to help Mallinson but most importantly to take his vision of Shangri-La back down to the suffering earth,
to the chaotic, hectic world of imminent mortality. The departure of
Conway, who seems intuitively aware of the inevitably Promethean
nature of his quest, from the timeless space of Shangri-La parallels
Robert Faehmel's dissolution of the timeless enchantment of the billiard-room ritual in Heinrich Böll's *Billiards at Half-Past Nine* (1959).

Robert Faehmel, the protagonist of the novel, strives initially to
transcend time not only by creating an ordered and orderly life but
also by achieving a "timeless" moment of aesthetic and intellectual

enchantment (from half-past nine until eleven in the morning) in the billiard-room at the Prinz Heinrich Hotel. Robert Faehmel creates a timeless enchanted moment through and in the formulaic, geometric configurations of the billiard balls which comprise a starry heaven.

Robert Faehmel escapes the negative, destructive images and memories of his past in this timeless moment of formulaic enchantment and formal detachment from everyday mortality, as Conway frees himself, at least temporarily, from the chaos of mortal existence in the aesthetic, cultural beauty of Shangri-La. Moreover, Conway, after having departed from Shangri-La, is able to return not only because his soul belongs intuitively to its aura of timelessness, but also because he retains in his mind an image, in the sense of Pound's conception of the image, of the lamasery world as an aesthetically enchanting emotional and intellectual complex in an instant of timelessness.

Robert Faehmel's apparent sublimation of compassion and feeling in the billiard-room ritual which did not allow the heart to become involved in the preservation of memory as formula is challenged and undermined when Schrella, Robert's brother-in-law, returns. Hugo notices the change which the arrival of Schrella introduces in the billiard-room ambience: "It seemed to him that the forms were less precise and the rhythm of the billiard balls disrupted. . . . Was it Schrella who had brought the perpetual present with him and broken the spell?" (266–67). Schrella's return is analogous to Mallinson's persuasion of Conway to leave Shangri-La. The crucial difference between these two experiences is that whereas the timeless enchantment of the billiard-room ritual is forever broken, Shangri-La remains a place of relatively timeless sanctuary to which Conway strives to return at the end. Schrella's return transforms the centripetal, self-directed, vitally individualistic aesthetic of Robert Faehmel into a profoundly centrifugal, aesthetically and emotionally vital moment of humanitarian awareness. Mallinson exerts a similar influence on Conway encouraging him to feel responsible for the welfare of others who were not suited to the aura and life-philosophy of Shangri-La.

According to Rutherford, Conway seems to be returning towards Shangri-La at the end of the novel. Perhaps this is because he realizes that only in the atmosphere of such a timeless, transcendent space can the sense of expansive timelessness which he has already achieved be perpetually renewed without the immediate encroachment of everyday mortality. Or perhaps because Conway feels that the world to which he has come down is not yet ready to appreciate and understand the message of Shangri-La which stresses the importance of developing a devotion to the preservation of the cultural and intellectual heritage of the world and of sustaining that devotion in a spirit of profoundly serene wisdom.

Although the High Lama of Shangri-La suggests that this mountain ambience can only check the flux of time and not halt it entirely, Conway perhaps desires to return to Shangri-La because he knows intuitively that it is a unique place, a place greatly superior to the aggressive, chaotic world of everyday mortality, which does offer an ambience of timelessness. Through the etherial tranquillity which permeates it, Shangri-La is able to preserve and refine this aura of timelessness. The silence that pervades Shangri-La is culturally dynamic and spiritually vital. Conway's attempt to return to Shangri-La parallels the transformation of diastolic to hermetic space in the narrative—for Conway realizes that the genius of Shangri-La derives to a considerable extent from its hermetically serene space.

Wordsworth's persona in Book 14 of *The Prelude* can envision the end of time through his experience of a diastolic space in the spirit of Romanticism. Despite the excesses of the French Revolution, or perhaps to some extent because of them, the romantic "I" conceives of the world as an openended venture, as a palpable space of unending possibilities. The creative persona who is open to this potential may appreciate more readily the diastolic space and time which he envisions. Conway, on the other hand, has experienced the misery and tragedy of a world war in all its terrifying and horrific immediacy. As a result, Conway is more inclined to seek a space which transcends the vicissitudes of everyday mortality, a space which is radiantly hermetic in its differentiation from the world whose cultural and intellectual significance it aspires to preserve.

Whether or not Conway does find his way back to the geographically remote Shangri-La, he has achieved his quest for a sense of timelessness. By participating devotedly and wholeheartedly in the world of Shangri-La Conway becomes forever an integral part of its serene timelessness. Conway's experience at Shangri-La is comparable to that of Hugo in *Billiards at Half-Past Nine* who, having been given a sense of eternity by participating in Robert Faehmel's enchanted moment of timelessness in the billiard-room, feels that he has always had it, that it has always signified an integral aspect of his inner being.

Conway's soul, the emotional, intellectual, and spiritual dimension of the self, will always be a significant aspect of the aura of Shangri-

La. As in the reciprocally vital interrelation of poet and spirit in Shelley's "Ode to the West Wind," Conway needs Shangri-La just as Shangri-La needs Conway and his serenely wise approach to life. Shangri-La may continue to exist without the direct presence of Conway, but it is Conway's spirit that will sustain and guide Shangri-La into an auspicious future. By asserting and reaffirming his conviction in the beauty, importance, and wisdom of the remote lamasery world, Conway enhances not only his own sense of timelessness but also the vitality of the timelessness and the capacity for perpetual renewal of Shangri-La.

Chapter 4

Thomas Mann

C. E. Williams begins the essay "Not an Inn, But an Hospital" by
stressing the autobiographical undertone of Thomas Mann's *The Magic
Mountain*:

> In the summer of 1912 Thomas Mann paid a visit to his wife who was under-
> going a short course of treatment in a Davos sanatorium. His experiences
> there inspired the idea of writing a humorous counterpart to the recently
> completed 'Death in Venice,' a satyr play to parody and offset the tragic
> novella. (37)

Williams proceeds to emphasize the connection between the emotional and spiritual adventure which the novel's protagonist, Hans
Castorp, undergoes and the tradition of the "Bildungsroman," the
novel of emotional, intellectual, and spiritual education. The education of Castorp, Williams argues, is achieved by the "process of
'Steigerung,' an alchemistic term implying purification, concentration,
and intensification. . . . The hero matures and gains a depth of insight which would have been out of the question in any other context"
(37). Castorp is receptive to numerous intellectual and spiritual influences and dimensions of the magic mountain environment, not the
least of which are the features of spatial and temporal expansiveness.

Hans Castorp's quest for the magic mountain, characterized by the
dynamic process of "Steigerung" (which is based on Goethe's perception of "Polarität" and "Steigerung"), derives its vitality from the following qualities, tendencies, or events: Castorp's familiarity with and
intuitive affinity for death; his adoption of the sanatorium world's value-
system; his emotional, intellectual, and spiritual attraction to images
of timeless, or seemingly timeless, continuity; his hermetically intense
discussions with Settembrini, among others, which lead to a greater
historical awareness; his own mythological vitality; his burgeoning

knowledge of and understanding of time; and his participation in the timeless harmony of nature.

Castorp develops early in his life an intuitive understanding of death, an instinctive appreciation of images of death. The most conspicuous memories of Castorp's parental home are associated with illness and death. The deaths of Castorp's mother, father, and grandfather within the space of only a few years is a tragic experience, although Mann describes this period in his protagonist's life as not being overwhelmingly painful. In his grandfather's house, where Castorp stays after the death of his parents, Castorp develops and strengthens a sense of tradition and continuity which is most effectively expressed through the symbol of the christening basin which exudes a sense of antiquity and timelessness.

This intuitive understanding of death in the "flatland" becomes an affinity for death on the magic mountain in the spirit of the sympathetic attitude towards death expressed by several German Romantic writers. Novalis asserts the necessity of physical illness for creative vitality. Friedrich Schlegel views illness as a spiritual force. E. T. A. Hoffman writes in "Councillor Krespel" of an artist whose physical weakness is the source of her creative genius, her stunningly beautiful voice, as well as of her ultimate demise. The awareness of illness not as something disgraceful but as the spiritual means to an intellectual and emotional awakening is found in some of Mann's early narratives, especially in "Little Herr Friedemann" and "A Weary Hour," and later in "Death in Venice."

The eight-year-old Hans Castorp is described as having a sensation of time as both flowing and persisting, of recurrence in continuity. The experience of a sense of timeless continuity is associated with Castorp's intuitive appreciation of death:

> As he listened to the great-great-great, he seemed to smell the cool, earthy air of the vault of St. Michael's or Saint Katherine's; the breath of regions where one went hat in hand, the head reverently bowed, walking weavingly on the tips of one's toes; seemed, too, to hear the remote and set-apart hush of those echoing places. (Mann 22)

Castorp's reverence for death is linked with his feeling of religious awe, as the timeless continuity which the repetition of "great" suggests.

Mann speaks of Castorp's familiarity with death at an early age and his mature response to such familiarity: "The sight was no longer strange, it was already familiar; and as on those earlier occasions, only in still greater degree, he bore himself with a responsible air, quite self-controlled" (26). Castorp sees death as a two-dimensional condition: on the one hand, it represents a holy and spiritual state, characterized by mournful beauty. On the other hand, it is a material and physical condition which has nothing spiritual about it.

As a child and young man Castorp reveals certain qualities which will later distinguish him as an appropriate member of the Berghof world. Of paramount importance is Castorp's intuitive familiarity with death. Castorp's difference from the "flatland" world to which he seems to belong so perfectly is suggested by his artistic talent, as undeveloped as it is and will remain. For example, at age fifteen Castorp produces a water-color of a graceful ship which shows artistic talent. Castorp, being peaceful and interested in a solid career, chooses, with encouragement from a family friend, to study ship-building. Perhaps he also senses that he may fulfill at least some of his artistic inclinations in such a career.

Another quality of Castorp which suggests that he may adapt well to the sanatorium world where he plans to take a short, three-week rest cure, is his penchant for mild pleasures and material comfort—he has respect for work but he does not like it. Such an attitude is reminiscent of the primary life-strategy of Hugh Conway in Hilton's *Lost Horizon*: "He was enjoying that pleasant mingling of physical ease and mental alertness which seemed to him, of all sensations, the most truly civilized" (85).

Castorp's journey to the Berghof Sanatorium in Switzerland foreshadows the tumultuousness, the timeless vitality of his sanatorium experience. As the journey from the flatland to the mountain culminates in a steep and steady climb that seems endless, Castorp's Berghof experience will be a "wild and rocky" (3) emotional and intellectual adventure. The description of Castorp's journey foregrounds the predominant importance of space—"space . . . possessed and wielded the powers we generally ascribe to time" (4).

The experience of novel and seemingly endless space leads Castorp to a sense of inner freedom: "Space, like time, engenders forgetfulness; but it does so by setting us bodily free from our surroundings and giving us back our primitive, unattached state" (4). Through his experience of a timeless space Castorp gains a profound sense of timelessness.

Such an ambience of timeless space is, of course, at the heart of the Berghof experience. The sanatorium world, like the world of Shangri-La in Hilton's *Lost Horizon*, achieves a sense of timelessness through its physical isolation from the everyday world. Not only does Castorp seem to appreciate the sense of time—the timelessness—which the Berghof maintains, but he also feels almost immediately comfortable speaking with Settembrini. Castorp assumes gradually, and without much difficulty, the carefree, almost Bohemian, approach to life and time at the sanatorium.

When Settembrini tells Castorp that he is bold to have come to the sanatorium, to have descended into the depths peopled by the vacant and idle dead, he seems to ascribe a mythological vitality to Castorp or perhaps just the potential to achieve such a mythological vitality. Settembrini also informs Castorp that the shortest unit of time in the sanatorium world is the month, implying that Castorp's intended three-week stay is not even worth measuring. In the ensuing conversation with Settembrini Castorp admits that he is not perhaps physically suited to his chosen career, for he feels really fit when he is doing nothing at all.

Victor Lange in "Thomas Mann the Novelist" describes the Berghof experience of Castorp as follows:

> Inescapably drawn into the rhythm of life and death, day and night, health and disease, waking and dreaming, musical transcendence and medical diagnosis, all of these soon felt and understood as inescapable polarities, Hans Castorp gradually gains an intense sense of self as well as a heightened perception of the intellectual and political convictions of Europe before 1914. (3)

Yet Castorp is not merely drawn into such a perpetual rhythm, for he shows instinctively, if not intuitively, a proclivity to participate in and to understand such a rhythm of seemingly irreconcilable oppositions.

Horst S. and Ingrid G. Daemmrich in *Spirals and Circles* interpret the "magic mountain" experience of Castorp in the following way:

> Hans Castorp moves during his exposure to learning experiences on the Magic Mountain within an infinite spiral of perception—understanding, objectified perception—enhanced understanding toward increasing self-insight and an understanding of the historical forces that shaped the modern world. (2:4)

They proceed to emphasize effectively not only the versatility and devotion but also the sense of liberation which characterize and motivate his learning process:

> Seen in its entirety, his education reveals the story of the human spirit's search for self-explication through the forms of Eros, reflection on nature, historical thinking, metaphysics, science, art, and magic. . . . The incessant dialogue

that transforms every observed phenomenon into a living substance propels Castorp from an embryonic stage upward on a spiral that liberates him spiritually. (2:6–7)

Hans Castorp's conversations and discussions with Settembrini signify not only his intellectual awakening; they also offer him a sense of timelessness. Later in the novel Castorp's appreciation and understanding of the intense intellectual exchanges and oppositions of Settembrini and Naphta are also timeless moments, moments when he seems doubly removed from mortality (removed from the physical and intellectual ambience of everyday reality), though Settembrini and Naphta often discuss the past or present state of the world.

Fritz Kaufmann in *Thomas Mann: The World as Will and Representation* argues that Thomas Mann, by placing Hans Castorp on the magic mountain, "lets him thus transcend the world of the plain . . . and, in a way, transcend himself as well" (97). Although Castorp does not reveal the silent heroism of Joachim "he becomes worthy of being chosen the hero of *The Magic Mountain* because he is venturesome enough to create himself" (98). Such an individual who attempts to create himself anew in a conspicuously different existential context and to rejuvenate and enhance his aesthetic and intellectual awareness shows a distinctive nobility of character.

Despite Settembrini's admonition to leave the Berghof because the environment does not seem to be conducive to him mentally or physically, Castorp intends to stay, not only because he feels he could develop and strengthen his intellectual vitality through Settembrini's guidance, but also because of his attraction for Claudia Chauchat. Moreover, Castorp feels a strange attraction to Albin's condition of careless, carefree indifference to society—Castorp experienced a wild wave of sweetness at the thought of Albin's being relieved of the burden of a respectable life. Castorp feels something of Albin's life-philosophy, especially when he is overwhelmed by the physical, atmospheric effects of the Berghof environment. For example, at one point Castorp describes himself as feeling extreme fatigue and also feeling as if he were dreaming and trying to awake from such a state but being unable to.

In one of his dreams Castorp encounters Hofrat Behrens, who says to him that he is not without talent for a heightened degree of oxidization. Behrens seems disappointed that Castorp will not give them one short year of service at the Berghof. Ultimately, however, one might argue that instead of taking his apprenticeship at the Hamburg ship-

building firm, Castorp takes it at the Berghof, giving Behrens considerably more than just one year of service.

In another dream during that same night Castorp envisions
Settembrini, whom he belittles as a hand-organ man. While Castorp
is deciding how to remove Settembrini from the scene, he experiences
a sudden epiphanic moment, a moment of personally vital revelation:
"he was unexpectedly vouchsafed a signal insight into the true nature
of time; it proved to be nothing more or less than a 'silent sister,' a
mercury column without degrees" (92). This passage is important not
only because it suggests that Castorp feels threatened occasionally by
Settembrini's intellectual prowess, but also because it emphasizes the
relativity of time, the notion that time is dependent on an individual's
perception and conception of its flux.

Such an understanding of time reinforces Castorp's previous phi-
losophizing about time when he stresses that the existential condition
of time depends on the individual's perception of the passage of time.
With respect to the measurement of time Castorp raises the question
how we can possibly measure anything about which we actually know
nothing, not even a single one of its properties. He proceeds to say
that time should flow evenly if it is to be measured. But actually it does
not flow evenly, though we like to assume that it does, for the sake of
convenience. Castorp concludes this reflection on time by asserting
that our units of measurement are purely arbitrary conventions.

Castorp achieves a sense of timelessness in the Berghof world because it possesses its own sense of time. Joachim, Castorp's cousin,
affirms this point when he claims that the seasons in the ambience of
the International Sanatorium Berghof are not especially distinct from
one another and are not dependent on the "flatland" calendar. The
Berghof landscape reveals an aura of timelessness by possessing a
perpetual immanence of snow. The consistent presence of significant
features of nature, as the existence of a regular schedule of activity,
produces a strong sense and undertone of timelessness in which
Castorp readily participates.

In the excursus on the sense of time in chapter four, Thomas Mann
offers further important reflections on the nature of time and on the
relation of habit and time:

> But what then is the cause of this relaxation, this slowing-down that takes
> place when one does the same thing for too long a time? It is not so much
> physical or mental fatigue or exhaustion. . . . It is rather something psychi-

cal; it means that the perception of time tends, through periods of unbroken uniformity, to fall away; the perception of time, so closely bound up with the consciousness of life that the one may not be weakened without the other suffering a sensible impairment. (104)

Monotony and repetition may contract and dissipate the larger time-units to nothing at all. At the end of this excursus on time Castorp, though he has been on the magic mountain only for a short while, says that it seems an eternity back to the time when he arrived.

Hans Castorp, perhaps because he is, like Hugh Conway in *Lost Horizon*, not instinctively aggressive or ambitious, enjoys the idea of a rest-cure—Castorp is described as having the capacity to sit without occupation for hours on end. Another reason for this capacity is that Castorp loves to see time spaciously before him—he enjoys the conception or sensation, or perhaps even illusion, of an ocean of time stretching endlessly before him.

Castorp develops a diastolic sense of time (a sense of the fluidity and openendedness of time) on the magic mountain in the world of the Berghof Sanatorium which becomes a hermetic sense of time upon his departure at the end of the novel to participate in the world war. He also develops a diastolic sense of space, especially in the section entitled "Snow" where he experiences the aura of an endless landscape. In contrast to Wordsworth's persona who achieves a diastolic sense of time through a diastolic sense of space (that is, space precedes time), Mann's protagonist attains a diastolic sense of space after developing an expansive sense of time (that is, time precedes space).

Castorp achieves an expansiveness of self in the spirit of the sublime of Longinus. In his *Analytical Inquiry into the Principles of Taste* Richard Payne Knight describes the theory of the sublime of Longinus as follows:

All sublime feelings are, according to Longinus, feelings of exultation and expansion of the mind, tending to rapture and enthusiasm; and whether they be excited by sympathy with external objects, or arise from the internal speculations of the mind, they are still of the same nature. In grasping at infinity the mind exercises these powers . . . of multiplying without end; and, in so doing, it expands and exalts itself, by which means its feelings and sentiments become sublime. (36)

Such a grasping at infinity is precisely what Mann's protagonist and Wordsworth's "majestic intellect" do in expanding and enriching the self.

W.E. Berendsohn in *Künstler und Kämpfer in Bewegter Zeit* described Hans Castorp as follows:

> Hans Castorp is neither a genius nor a person significant for his achievements, nor is he a naive simpleton. Curiosity and a thirst for knowledge are peculiar to him and he loves to reflect on everything that crosses his path. Very early he questions the meaning of life, but not actively, not passionately searching. He is not a grail seeker; rather, a passive yet very attentive observer and listener in life's theatre with its changing repertoire. (73)

Although he is not a grail seeker in the medieval tradition, is Castorp not perhaps a modern seeker of the grail of "timelessness?" Are not the qualities of curiosity and a thirst for knowledge essential to such a seeker after "Aion"? Cartorp's "grail-seeking" quest is enhanced not only by his profound simplicity and clarity of thought but also by the fact that he may remain at the sanatorium for as long as he wishes to.

Castorp also seems to experience a sense of timelessness through music. Settembrini's discussion of music offers an insight into the capacity of music to express or reinforce a sense of timelessness. Settembrini, though preferring the word to music, says that music through its life-enhancing method of measuring time provides a sense of spiritual awareness and value to the passage of time. As part of its positive dimension, music quickens time, it stimulates us to the finest, fullest enjoyment of time.

On the other hand, music may also have an opposite and, in Settembrini's view, negative effect. For music may act like an opiate on us producing lethargy, inertia, and inaction. Settembrini claims that music is politically suspect because it is equivocal—it can lead either to spiritual-emotional awareness or to lethargy. One might argue that either aspect of music may encourage the development of a sense of timelessness, but especially the second. For in its narcotic effect, in its encouragement to lethargy, music causes time to slow down, or be suspended. A piece of music has its own inner time which replaces the normal flux of time—when one is absorbed in or captivated by a piece of music, external time ceases to exist. The individual establishes his own sense of time from the inner time of the music.

Castorp also experiences a strong sense of Berghof timelessness when he gets a cold and a slight fever. The fact that he has become ill affirms Castorp's instinctive association with the sanatorium world. That Castorp "belongs" to the Berghof ambience is reinforced by

Behrens who claims that he senses initially that Hans was one of them. Castorp tries to persuade his fellow sanatorium residents that his fever doesn't mean anything, but they also sense that he belongs to the Berghof. The sense of timelessness which Castorp experiences when he is sick is emphasized in the section "Soup-Everlasting" which opens chapter five. The statement is made that when a sick person spends time in bed, it is a continuous present, an everlastingness. Soup-everlasting, the everlasting midday broth, symbolizes this in itself and as a primordial fluid continuum.

Castorp's sense of timelessness when he is sick is reinforced by the fact that he is isolated not only from the Berghof society but also from the flatland community, from the world of everyday reality down below. Castorp responds positively and negatively to this sense of timelessness. The splendidly serene isolation pleases and disturbs him. Sometimes he misses the contact with his fellow Berghof residents. Castorp is grateful to Settembrini who, through his discussions, has filled the time for him, has given time content. Castorp even says that he almost wishes to keep his fever so he can continue to have the privilege of listening to Settembrini.

Settembrini emphasizes to Castorp the importance of his motto "Placet experiri." Henry Hatfield in *From The Magic Mountain: Mann's Later Masterpieces* claims that Castorp, in appreciating the significance of Settembrini's motto, demonstrates Nietzche's double perspective: "Conservative yet daring, he accepts the traditional 'Respice finem' (Think of the end) but corrects it with the Goethean 'Remember to live'" (65). In experiencing such a metaphysical tension Castorp heightens his capacity for intellectual development, for the intellectual awareness which he is eager to strive for and achieve and the guide for which Settembrini is more than willing to be.

Settembrini gives Castorp the sense of experiencing a vital, a profound timelessness by enhancing his self-awareness. For example, Settembrini suggests that Castorp's early and repeated contact with death developed in him a sensitivity to the harshness and cruelty of the world. Castorp acknowledges that he never would have experienced an intellectually aware timelessness if it had not been for Settembrini. Castorp supports his own contention that sensitivity and sensibility derive at least to some extent, if not to a considerable extent, from a sensitivity for death, or a degree of ill health, or both, by saying that if he had met Settembrini down below he would not have understood.

That is, although Castorp had developed a relatively vital sensitivity for death and for "otherness," such sensitivity could only have matured in the sanatorium environment, in an environment isolated from, if not disdained by and disdainful of, everyday reality and its temporal limitations. One might even argue, in conjunction with the thesis that the protagonist was fated to come to the Berghof Sanatorium, that Castorp sensed inwardly as a young man that he needed to escape from the shallowness, the superficiality, the cruelty, and the ruthlessness of the professional and social environment of everyday reality.

The section "Soup-Everlasting" speaks of an inner tension in the flow of time: "each day . . . never varied . . . and which, in its abiding uniformity, could not be said either to pass too fast or to hang too heavy on the hands" (189). Because of such seeming uniformity, because of the apparently pervasive regularity of Berghof time, Castorp feels occasionally that he does not have enough time to commune with his own thoughts. Despite the negative undertone which such uniformity may suggest, this condition also contributes to and leads into the implication of the mythological vitality of the protagonist.

When Castorp is sick and bed-ridden, he senses that each day fuses indistinguishably with the next, that the traditional parts of the day coalesce into a temporal oasis, wasteland, or abyss of everything or nothing:

> The day, artificially shortened, broken into small bits, had literally crumbled in his hands and was reduced to nothing: he remarked it to himself with a start—or, at any rate, he did at least remark; for to shudder at it was foreign to his years. It seemed to him that from the beginning of time he had been lying and looking thus. (192)

Such a passage evokes the image of a divine-like figure, a Promethean personality, in control of time. In assuming an emotional, intellectual, and psychological posture of timeless vitality, Castorp presents himself as a mythological force of hermetic wisdom.

In the section "Sudden Enlightenment" Castorp not only observes Joachim in the X-ray machine in an eye-opening, mind-expanding experience, but he also becomes poignantly aware of his own mortality. Hans Castorp looks at his own hand and envisions that he is looking into his own grave: "The process of decay was forestalled by the powers of the light-ray, the flesh in which he walked disintegrated, annihilated, dissolved in vacant mist, and there within it was the finely turned skeleton of his own hand" (218). Castorp's awareness of his mortality culminates in the statement: "With the eyes of his Tienappel ancestress, penetrating, prophetic eyes, he gazed at this familiar part of his own body, and for the first time in his life he understood that he would die" (218–19). It is especially significant that Castorp's face wears the same expression at this realization that it has when he listens to music: "a little dull, sleepy and pious, his mouth half open, his head inclined toward the shoulder" (219).

Perhaps partially as a self-fortifying response to the sudden awareness of his mortality Castorp writes a declaration of independence from the "flatland" mentality. In stressing that the conceptions of time in the Berghof world are different from those down below, the novice-engineer implies his familiarity with different temporal conceptions and strategies, perhaps even with time itself. By writing this letter saying that he must prolong his Berghof sojourn, Castorp reaffirms his sense of timelessness, an existential condition to be strongly differentiated from the imminent and pervasive mortality of the flatland. Castorp supports his experience of timelessness by articulating it so effectively. Yet Mann, for whom writing was an arduous and challenging task, does not wish us to think that Castorp could write with ease without paying a price for "plucking a leaf off the laurel-tree of art"— and not surprisingly, Castorp speaks of the strain he feels having completed the letter.

The natural environment plays a conspicuously significant role in the depiction of the Berghof ambience. It is not the irrational, cataclysmic power of nature which Settembrini, in the spirit of Voltaire's outrage with respect to the Lisbon earthquake of 1755, praises and which, by its tempestuous and violent aspect, would inevitably undermine a viable sense of timelessness. Rather, it is the serene, tranquil dimension of the mountain landscape which offers the most salient reinforcement of an aura of timelessness.

For example, in the section "Humaniora" atmosphere-enhancing nature is described:

> The sky above the valley was a deep southern blue and the pastures beneath, with the cattle tracks running across and across them, still a lively green. From the rugged slopes came the sound of cowbells; the peaceful, simple, melodious tintinnabulation came floating unbroken through the quiet, thin, empty air, enhancing the mood of solemnity that broods over the valley heights. (251)

One of the most important aspects of the aura of timelessness which Castorp tries, consciously as well as unconsciously, to sustain, is such a mood of solemnity. Such a mood is intimately related to his intuitive familiarity with death and the atmosphere of death he experienced as a child and young man.

In the following section "Research" Castorp preserves his increasingly more resilient Berghof sense of timelessness, which may perhaps be described as atemporality, by not celebrating the Christmas season with his family. Christmas represents a temporal landmark, "a fulcrum or a vaulting-pole with which to leap over empty intervening spaces" (270). Castorp seems not to cherish the Christmas holiday because it undermines the fluidity of Berghof time and challenges the continuum of timelessness which is so important to him.

What Castorp says about life in the same section is noteworthy because it may apply symbolically to his experience and interpretation of timelessness as well. Castorp tries to define life as not only as "the warmth generated by a form-preserving instability" (257), but also as "the existence of the actually impossible-to-exist, of a "half-sweet, half-painful balancing . . . in this restricted and feverish process of decay and renewal upon the point of existence" (275–76).

Might we not say the same about Castorp's condition of timelessness? Is it not an inner warmth generated by a provisional instability, a necessarily inevitable tension of matter and form? Does it not signify the impossible-to-exist, a half-sweet, half-painful balancing at the fragile edge of life and death? Timelessness, the experience of the timeless moment and a concatenation of timeless moments, was neither life nor death, but a threshold phenomenon. Castorp's experience of timelessness depends on the presence of an inner tension between life and death and on the provisional unity of such opposing forces.

Another dimension of Castorp's sense of timelessness is that he does not keep inward count of the time. Instead he tells time by the sensations which the season arouses: "He had not heeded the silent entry of the tenth month, but he was arrested by its appeal to the senses, this glowing heat that concealed the frost within and beneath it" (226).

Settembrini appears to play an ambivalent role in Castorp's quest for timelessness. On the one hand, his intellectual exchanges with Castorp help to give his young disciple a sense of timelessness. On the other hand, Settembrini warns Castorp to be wary of the Eastern carelessness and recklessness with respect to time, admonishing him that there is something frightful in the way he flings the months about. Settembrini is concerned not only about the undue influence of East-

ern ideas on his young protege, but also about the potentially dangerous influence of that symbol of irrationality, intellectual lethargy, and
sensuality, Claudia Chauchat.

Settembrini argues that the Russians are so reckless with time because they are a people of seemingly endless space. In contrast,
Settembrini asserts that the Europeans, because of limited space, must
be economical with time. Settembrini ends this line of argument by
reasserting part of the rationalist's credo: "Time is a gift of God, given
to man that he might use it—use it, Engineer, to serve the advance-
ment of humanity" (243).

As a corollary to this point Fritz Kaufmann argues that Castorp
abandons the ties and privileges of the bourgeois world, of the nineteenth-century Buddenbrooks society, in the quest for a higher realm
of social consciousness and existence "which is ultimately not Hans
Castorp's mystical trance but the true world-citizenship, the loyalty to
earth and man, for which he is secretly fitted by his education on the
magic mountain" (101).

It is interesting that most of the reading at the Berghof is done by
the new-comers and the "short-timers," for the long-term patients
"had long learned to kill time without mental effort or means of distraction, by dint of a certain inner virtuosity they came to possess"
(272). Castorp, however, reads extensively. After finishing *Ocean
Steamships*, his immediate intellectual connection with the "flatland,"
Castorp reads books on scientific engineering and ship-building, which
he ordered from home. Then he orders books from the village on
anatomy, physiology, and biology. Such reading is important because
it underlines Castorp's fascination with life and its sacred and impure
mysteries. Castorp's endeavor to understand these mysteries is significant not only because it underscores the difference between the "enchanted," isolated Berghof world and the world down below, but also
because it speaks of the essential dualism in human nature and existence which is crucial to the experience of timelessness.

Castorp's awareness of and reverence for solemnity, intimately linked
to his concern for timelessness, is revitalized in the section entitled
"The Dance of Death." Castorp evokes here the image of a caretaker
which places him above the daily anguish of many of his fellow Berghof
residents and gives him a semblance of timelessness. In asserting his
disagreement with the attempt of the Berghof authority to spare the
resident-patients who are not near death from the misery and dying of
the difficult cases, Castorp says that he has decided to concern himself

more in the future with the severe cases and the moribund. Such a strategy might suggest that Castorp is trying to fulfill his role as "caretaker"—however, it might also imply a self-imposed challenge to his quest for timelessness. Perhaps this is an initial sign of Castorp's self-sacrificial, heroic attitude which will ultimately lead him back to the military cataclysm in the flatland at the end of the novel.

When Castorp sends flowers to some fatally ill people at the Berghof, Settembrini says to him that he has the more gifted, if also the more exposed nature, in contrast with Joachim. Settembrini speaks of Castorp as life's delicate child. Castorp, perhaps partially to satisfy a spiritual craving to take suffering and death seriously, though certainly also as a humanitarian gesture, likes to occupy himself with the "children of death." As a result of such Good Samaritan-spirited activity, visiting and spending time with seriously ill patients, Castorp has become more serious and reflective—or perhaps one should say that the sanatorium environment has inspired his potential for contemplation and seriousness and encouraged such a significant humanistically motivated capacity to blossom and thrive. As Henry Hatfield astutely points out, the visits which Hans makes to the dying not only show his fascination with death, they also suggest "that truly felt knowledge of death makes a person more humane" (43).

Castorp and Joachim take one of the dying patients, Karen, to the Platz theater to view a pageant of life as well as to the cemetery, which contains mostly graves of people who died when they were young, who were usually not more than twenty years old. The cemetery visit constitutes a sobering experience; yet, it is also a symbolic reinforcement of the aura and the tone of the sanatorium world—a sense of everlasting peace, a sense of timelessness, of timeless serenity, of a deep and profound stillness.

Although Castorp desires solemnity and respect for death, he thinks that it is quite proper to celebrate the holidays of the world below at the Berghof. Settembrini is disturbed to hear Castorp speaking with such frivolity about the Berghof entertainment, perhaps because he senses the ever-present influence of the Eastern life-philosophy. Claudia's departure might diminish such an influence; but Claudia's departure is perhaps most important because it upsets the sense of enchantment, of painfully sweet enchantment, which Castorp feels in her presence, whether direct or indirect. One might also argue that her departure may potentially solidify Castorp's sense of timelessness because it demonstrates his persistent existence at the sanatorium despite the manifold vicissitudes of life and death.

In contrast to the sense of timelessness of the protagonist, Mann speaks of the changes which time has brought about in the Berghof world. One mark of temporal change is the presence of gaps at various tables in the dining-room seating. Mann explains that the gaps are due not only to choice but also to the presence, if not the omnipresence, of death.

Another prominent change that occurs at this time and that is described in the section "Changes" is the gradual, problematic emergence of spring. Mann presents the birth of spring as a difficult and strained process of overcoming the persistent presence and vitality of winter. Such determination reflects and reinforces the courageous persistence of the Berghof inmates in fighting death. Finally, spring breaks through, infusing the solemnity of the Berghof environment with a radiantly vital ray of hope. However, the arrival of spring also suggests mortality, the inevitable flux of time which is less prominent when there is eternal snow on the mountain.

Chapter six of *The Magic Mountain* begins with several interesting reflections on time. Time is a mystery and a figment—it is all-powerful, conditioning the external world of everyday reality. The notion of time is important because it necessitates and reinforces the idea of change. In speculating about the nature of time, about infinity and eternity, about conceptions of distance, movement, and change, Castorp shows not only that his intellectual awareness is being sharpened and strengthened but also that he possesses the inner dedication to the conception of time to assume the role of quester for a sense of timelessness.

Castorp's interest in comprehending the breadth of knowledge demonstrates further the vitality of his intellectual awakening and development. Not only does he make progress in his botanical systematization, for beneath each specimen in his herbarium he carefully inscribes the Latin name in ornamental lettering, but he has also gained knowledge of the zodiac and of ancient civilizations.

Castorp, like his mentor, is strongly interested in the cultural and intellectual development of humankind. He thinks of the Chaldeans, for example, and how in their time they gazed at the stars and made verses about them. Being on the magic mountain allows Castorp to conceive and perceive ideas about humanity which are novel to him. Moreover, like Goethe's Wilhelm Meister, who enters a new world that inspires his sense of awe and his capacity for emotional-intellectual assimilation, Castorp gains a comprehensive understanding of human development. Such a perspective invigorates his humanistically ecumenical acceptance of the complexity of the human condition: "You have to take humanity as it is; but even so I find it magnificent" (370).

In this same passage Castorp reveals again his strong awareness of the flux of time and his critical response to the normative perception of time. Castorp proceeds to call seasonal demarcations a practical joke—namely, that spring begins at the beginning of winter and autumn at the beginning of summer. He says one feels that one is being fooled, led around in a circle with one's vision fixed on something that is really a moving point: "For the circle consists of nothing but such transitional points without any extent whatever; the curvature is incommensurable, there is no duration of motion, and eternity turns out to be not 'straight ahead' but 'merry-go-round'" (370–71). This statement effectively describes Castorp's experience of and sensation of timelessness, for his most vital experience on the magic mountain is dependent upon such transitional points and transitory enchanted moments.

Castorp reflects upon the significance of the feast of the solstice—midsummer night. He wonders whether this day marked a celebration because from then on the world "went down into the dark" (371) or because "it had up till then gone uphill, and now the turning-point was reached" (371). Castorp sees this day not only as a feast celebrating past joy and positive feeling and signifying the first summer night, the night with which autumn begins, but also as a transitional moment, a moment of cosmic and cosmological conflict, of emotional, intellectual, and spiritual tension, described as the fleeting moment of midsummer night and midsummer madness, the confluence of tears and laughter. The oxymoronic quality of the language Castorp uses to express the vitality of the solstice moment is noteworthy because it reflects the powerful inner tension of the moment culminating in tragic joy and triumphant sadness.

Helmut Koopmann argues in *Thomas Mann* that Hans Castorp represents a mediating figure between Settembrini and Naphta, a figure sustaining the vitality of "die Mitte," which is the bourgeois realm transferred to new heights of feeling and thought. Referring to Castorp's critical commentary on the conflict between Settembrini and Naphta, representing Western and Eastern world-views respectively, Koopmann writes that Castorp aspires to signify the position of the middle-class and moderation (105).

In the spirit of his role as an intellectually aware spectator of the world, Castorp functions effectively as a mediator between Settembrini and Naphta. In arguing for clarity—he feels that the two antagonists sometimes seem to be confused in presenting their views on the world order—Castorp shows his willingness to reconcile the emotional and intellectual tensions in the otherwise serene mountain air. Castorp not only mediates but he also disregards the admonitions of Settembrini to avoid contact with Naphta. Such a strategy suggests that Castorp, as much as he respects Settembrini, is determined to develop and enrich his intellectual awareness at all costs, perhaps in the tradition of Gustav Aschenbach in "Death in Venice," who consecrates himself completely to the challenge of developing his aesthetic awareness and vitality.

Castorp's potential as a mediating spirit is linked to his capacity to represent the universal human condition, to universalize the human spirit. Of this capacity Kaufmann writes:

> Although Hans Castorp is not a poet, he nonetheless evinces a trait belonging to a poet's very essence, namely pure receptivity. In this substratum of the artistic a certain satisfaction is already given to man's yearning to unite his individual life with the life of the universe. (105)

Kaufmann proceeds to assert that just as art may represent the particular in its universal significance, so Castorp's receptivity to diverse ideas and sensations enables him to gain a sense of universality in his inner being.

In "Choler, And Worse" Castorp did not look forward to his first anniversary at the sanatorium. With such an indifferent attitude Castorp shows that he has become part of the Berghof world. For there was an unwritten rule, an aspect of the oral tradition of the sanatorium, that such an anniversary would not be celebrated. Most Berghof residents accord the anniversary of their arrival a profound silence: "They let it slip past, perhaps they actually managed to forget it, and they might be confident that no one else would remember" (413). Perhaps they react in such a way because they wish to preserve at least a semblance of continuity with their pre-Berghof lives; or perhaps they feel a more profound sense of timelessness if they view their lives as a smoothly flowing temporal continuum.

Mann also points out that although the veteran Berghof residents are aware of the general passage of time, they are not inclined to celebrate their private time. Yet there seems to be a contradiction here, for several lines earlier Mann says that the old inhabitants celebrated not only their private anniversaries but also the events which marked the recurrent rhythms of the year. Mann seems to resolve this textual tension when he writes: "The settled citizens preferred the unmeasured, the eternal, the day that was for ever the same" (413). Perhaps the settled citizens do not wish to celebrate and remember the anniversary of their arrival at the Berghof because such an event would remind them of a time and a world which they would like to forget.

Castorp's sense of timelessness is certainly enhanced by the ethereal serenity of the natural environment around the international sanatorium. But the nature of this mountain landscape may also easily undermine such a sense of timelessness. Castorp argues that human needs are in harmony with the larger, the fundamental facts of nature. He contrasts the salutary effect of nature down below where one is glad to see summer and winter come again because the old summer or winter lie far enough in the past and the problematic nature at the Berghof where there are no proper seasons, but only summer days and winter days all mixed up together. Moreover, when the new winter arrives, it really is not new, but the same old winter all the time. In such a statement Castorp seems to suggest that one primary dimension of the Berghof timelessness, namely, that which derives from old, regurgitated seasons, is not an affirmative and growthful timelessness. This negative sense of timelessness is countered simultaneously by the positive sense of timelessness characterized by a profound serenity and a feeling of having a superabundance of "time."

The relatively strong sense of timelessness which Castorp had achieved prior to his discussion with Joachim about nature and prior to Joachim's departure is further undermined when Castorp is given a place at a new table in the dining room, at Settembrini's table. Moreover, Castorp receives a visit from the "flatland"—his uncle, James Tienappel, comes to see how he is progressing. Tienappel reveals a quality we have also seen in Castorp: in his own sphere, in Hamburg, he is the practical businessman. Outside this sphere he displays a friendly readiness to step outside his own personality. Tienappel leaves suddenly after only a few days, most likely because he sensed that a longer stay would require a significant readjustment to life in the flatland.

Tienappel's departure from the Berghof ended the endeavor of the flatland to recover its lost Hans Castorp. Castorp realizes that this moment signified a crisis in the relations between himself and the world below. This moment of realization represents for Castorp "the consummation of freedom—the thought of which had gradually ceased to make him shudder" (440). Castorp, the increasingly wise and emotionally and intellectually aware protagonist, is so much at home in the Berghof ambience that he feels no inclination or compulsion to leave. Perhaps Castorp's approach is somewhat like that of Naphta who has been at the Berghof for six years, so that his presence is "no longer so much a cure as a fixed condition of existence, a residence for life in a rarefied atmosphere" (447).

In the section "Snow" of chapter six Castorp achieves an epiphanic moment, a profound moment of awareness about life and time. The Berghof environment has a monstrous snowfall—the snow covers everything, as if to reinforce the isolation of the Berghof from the world. Castorp is enchanted by the magical quality of this snowy world, finding this ambience similar to life at the seashore: "the monotony of the scene was in both cases profound. The snow, so deep, so light, so dry and spotless, was the sand of down below" (473).

In his essay "'Bildung' in The Magic Mountain" W. H. Bruford affirms the connection for Mann between the expansiveness of the sea and the endlessness of the mountain-snow. Thomas Mann said that the sea was one element of nature that always fascinated him: "The sea is not a landscape, it is something that brings us face to face with eternity, with nothingness and death, a metaphysical dream, and to stand in the thin air of the regions of eternal snow is a very similar experience" (84).

Castorp goes skiing to admire the natural beauty of these wintry heights which are described as being enveloped in a deathly stillness which arouses feelings of awe similar to those one might feel along the edge of the sea. Castorp also embarks on this adventure to search, perhaps more unconsciously than consciously, for the intangible, the mysterious, a secret of life and of timelessness. With his skis Castorp explores ever more barren regions—he finds the complete solitude which he craves. Yet, he is also aware of the potential danger of elemental nature.

The figure of Castorp in this episode is analogous to the lonely, isolated figures in several of Caspar David Friedrich's paintings—for example, in Monk By the Sea (1809), The Abbey (1810), or Cross in the Woods (1812). In these paintings, the figure, invariably and inevitably dwarfed by the landscape, confronts a seemingly inhospitable, elemental, and primeval nature. Castorp is differentiated from the personae in Friedrich's paintings in that he is and would not be content with the emotional-spiritual unity or continuity with nature which they

appear to achieve. Nature for Castorp does not constitute a complementary dimension in the world of eternal flux. Nature is always either
dominant over or supplementary to Castorp and his strategy, gradually and perhaps even painstakingly nurtured at the Berghof, of consistent intellectual inquiry.

In feeling a religious awe for nature, Castorp senses the fascination
of venturing just so far into the unknown that the adventure touched
on the perilous. In his narrow, hypercivilized breast Hans Castorp
cherished a sense of kinship with the elements—his exploration of the
elemental solitude and vastness of nature is comparable to his intellectual adventures with Settembrini and Naphta. In both instances he
feels a sense of association with his "antagonists," but he also feels a
respectful critical distance from them.

As in his mediating role in the intense exchanges between
Settembrini and Naphta, so in his exploration of nature Castorp assumes a Faustian quality. Castorp climbs up high into the mountains,
into the snowy haze, without a definite destination, ever higher into
the "upper regions blended with a sky no less misty-white than they"
(478). Does this signify Castorp's ascent into the abyss? Castorp's
ambiguous feelings are rejuvenated—he is oppressed by the monstrous
solitude, yet he is proud to have ventured so far. In his exploration
Castorp does not just view nature with reverential awe—he reflects on
the forms of nature, on nature's aesthetic and physical vitality.

Castorp's experience of the "magic mountain" and his dream-
vision in the "Snow" episode are prefigured by Friedrich Schiller's
visionary experience on the "magic mountain" in "Der Spaziergang."

Schiller finds aesthetic, emotional, and intellectual rejuvenation in
the presence of the "magic mountain" in "Der Spaziergang." Schiller's
"Ich" in "Der Spaziergang," as Castorp in the "Snow" adventure, exists at the threshold of two emotional and physical antitheses or extremes, between "Schwindeln" and "Schaudern" as between "Höh"
and "Tiefe," and symbolically between life and death. Yet, this is an
existential tension which resolves itself in the poet's conception of the
"Äther" as a dynamic, fluid unity and in his anticipation of following
the continuity of the trellised path.

Schiller's ascension of the mountain is an occasion to comprehend
in his field of artistic vision the expansiveness of the world of humankind and of nature. His contemplation of the growth of human civilization is generated by a sense of dynamic space, by the spatial metaphor of "ein schimmernder Streif, die länderverknüpfende Strasse."

After a consideration of the constructive, positive evolution of the human spirit in conjunction with divine assistance, Schiller's "Ich" proceeds to reflect upon the dark, destructive aspects of humanity as well. As Castorp in his dream-vision on the mountain, so Schiller's "Ich" experiences an intellectual and aesthetic adventure that encompasses polarities of human existence and resolves them ultimately in the unified conception of the innately harmonious, eternal cyclicality of nature.

The sense of youthfulness and vernal vitality culminating the poem, which reinforces the rejuvenation of the "Ich" in this "magic mountain" experience embracing and fusing life and death as well as dream and reality, signifies not only the emotional and intellectual condition of the "Ich" but also the spiritual aura of Nature. For the "Ich" is not only reenergized in the purifying presence of Nature, he is also aware of participating in the eternal cyclicality of the natural world. The poem concludes with an image of the expansiveness of time, not only in the sense of the eternal vitality of nature and of humankind, but also in the realization that the congenial past may infuse inspirationally the present, represented by the sun of Homer smiling upon the present.

In contrast to Castorp who internalizes a sense of time before an awareness of space, Schiller's "Ich," like Wordsworth's poetic voice in *The Prelude*, achieves a sense of the expansiveness of space before he attains a sense of the expansiveness of time. Despite this difference, I would argue that Schiller's "Ich" and Castorp ultimately achieve similar "magic mountain" experiences. What they share are an instinctive awareness of the threshold nature of the "magic mountain" ambience, a profound sense of personal revitalization after confronting heroically the primeval solitudes of the mountain wilderness, a renewed commitment to the potential dignity and vitality of life and humanity, and a visionary capacity that not only apprehends the inextricable relation of life and death, but also intuits the connections and tensions between the conceptions of spatial and temporal expansiveness.

The inspirational power of the sublime landscape, expressed by Thomas Gray in his letters describing his visit to the Grande Chartreuse in 1739, is felt as well by Castorp in his magic mountain context. Gray writes: "I do not remember to have gone ten paces without an exclamation, that there was no restraining: not a precipice, not a torrent, not a cliff, but is pregnant with religion and poetry" (70).

Though Gray perceives the power of the intellectual and spiritual breadth of the majestic intellect primarily in nature, Mann, as the Wordsworth of *The Prelude*, conceives it in the mind and in nature.

Gray, in describing his experience in the mountainous landscape, also speaks of seeing spirits at noon and sensing the presence of death perpetually before his eyes. The following passage exemplifies Gray's sense of the mountain adventure as a threshold experience between life and death: "It is six miles to the top; the road runs winding up it, commonly not six feet broad; on the one hand is the rock, with woods of pine-trees hanging overhead; on the other, a monstrous precipice . . . at the bottom of which rolls a torrent" (62). Gray's depiction of the mountain experience as signifying the fragile edge of life and death anticipates the mountain experiences of Wordsworth, Arnold, Hilton, and Mann, all of whom portray the sublime ascent and subsequent descent as an interaction and fusion of gloom and glory.

This awareness of the threshold nature of the magic mountain experience is reinforced by Gray's sense (affirmed in their own way by the protagonists in Mann's *The Magic Mountain*, Wordsworth's *The Prelude*, Arnold's "Stanzas from the Grande Chartreuse," and Hilton's *Lost Horizon*) of being caught between the beautiful and the sublime. Kant says that whereas the sublime is signified by boundlessness, the beautiful is characterized by form and limits. Kant goes on to say that the sublime represents a dynamic state of mind while the beautiful is observed by a mind at rest. Kant, in locating the sublime within the creative mind, says that objects such as mountain peaks, chasms, or high waterfalls "raise the energies of the soul above their accustomed height, and discover in us a faculty of resistance of a quite different kind, which gives us courage to measure ourselves against the apparent almightiness of nature" (125).

For Mann's protagonist the magic mountain is a threshold space at the fragile edge of time and eternity, life and death, the beautiful and the sublime. As for Hilton, so for Mann the mountain environment is a place of intellectual vitality but without the same motivation. Hilton's Shangri-La aims to preserve the cultural heritage of human civilization in anticipation of a future international cataclysm. Mann's Berghof Sanatorium offers intellectual stimulation not only as a distraction, a diversion from the pervasive aura of death and decay but also as a foundation for the emotional, intellectual, and spiritual expansion of the self in its attempt to cultivate a more insightful understanding of humanity.

In *Thomas Mann: Profile and Perspectives* Andre von Gronicka writes of Castorp's quest for timelessness: "In the snowswept wilderness of his 'Munsalvasche,' his 'wild mountain,' in the grip of death, at a moment of heightened perception, Castorp finds the strength to break death's fatal fascination and to dedicate himself to life, kindliness and love" (139). Gronicka emphasizes the significance of the protagonist's striving to transcend death by committing himself to the ideal of a new humanism which would elevate the dignity of life above the dignity of death.

Castorp experiences a vital sense of freedom among the snowy heights: "he rejoiced in his freedom of motion, his feet were like wings" (480). Such a sense of freedom encourages Castorp to take further risks. He continues further into the wild and deepening silence even though the "gathering darkness was sinking down over the region like a veil, and heightening his inner apprehension until it presently passed into actual fear" (481). Castorp admits his enjoyment of such freedom in saying that he had set out to lose his way. He wishes to make full use of his time in this wandering, as he perhaps does not want to make fully active use of his time at the Berghof. This moment of confronting the profundity and power of nature represents perhaps Castorp's ultimate challenge to himself and his ultimate assertion of the freedom of the soul.

The image of the seven-league slippers is important not only because of its inherently enchanted, romantic vitality but also because it suggests the capacity of the protagonist to cover great spaces, great expanses of space, easily, a feat beyond the capability of most, if not all, mortals. The experience of spatial expansiveness, of diastolic spatiality, contributes to and reinforces Castorp's sense of timelessness. As in the Berghof environment there is a dream-like quality to the experience of timelessness which makes it all the more etherial and vital.

The challenge of this epiphanic moment intensifies in the breaking of the storm. Castorp feels fatigue and excitement in challenging the elemental forces of nature, in trying to find his way out of the storm, just as he does after a colloquy with Settembrini and Naphta. Castorp reinforces the self-challenge by saying that he does not want to be covered up and conquered by the "hexagonal symmetricality" (485), in other words, by an objective, formal nature, whose power is not generated by a vital principle of life. Castorp's resistance of the storm symbolizes his attempt to remain intellectually alive. He makes an extraordinary effort to persevere. Although he could see nothing and despite the weight of the cold on his limbs, he continues to struggle forward. Castorp finds the illusion of shelter at the hut—perhaps he is able to overcome the storm, as he overcomes mortality and time, because he preserves and strengthens a self-generated intellectual and spiritual power.

At the climax of "Snow" Castorp senses a presence in nature as powerful as the presence that disturbs Wordsworth's persona in "Tintern Abbey" with the joy of elevated thoughts who feels

> a sense sublime
> Of something far more deeply interfused,
> Whose dwelling is the light of setting suns, . . .
> A motion and a spirit, that impels
> All thinking things, all objects of all thought,
> And rolls through all things. (95–102)

Such a "sense sublime" is analogous to the spirit of transcendent awareness which culminates Castorp's experience in "Snow." Castorp's outward-directed awareness of participating in the "motion" and "spirit" of the universe is described insightfully by Horst S. and Ingrid G. Daemmrich in *Spirals and Circles* as follows: "He reaches the decision to establish a productive relation with the world by reconciling spiritual existence with a reverence for the dynamic forces of nature" (2:7).

Castorp, as Wordsworth's persona in "Tintern Abbey," experiences a motion and a spirit that pervades all dimensions of his "Snow" adventure. For example, one of the most interesting and intriguing dimensions of the "Snow" section is Castorp's dream of a southern climate filled with images of life, of loveliness, and of vitality. Yet, there is also a temple where two old women are dismembering a child. This intense perceptual moment signifies the heightened intellectual and spiritual awareness of Castorp—life and death are part of each other's domain, inevitably and necessarily. Castorp understands the inner tension of this lovely and horrible dream.

In interpreting the dream, or vision, from a Jungian perspective, Castorp affirms the vitality of his own quest for knowledge, which is simultaneously his quest for timelessness: "We dream anonymously and communally, if each after his fashion. The great soul of which we are a part may dream through us, in our manner of dreaming, its own secret-dreams" (495). Castorp says he still feels the intensity of his dream, the horror of the sacrifice as well as the happiness at the sight of the lovely creatures. He claims that he has gained the right to dream such expressionistically realistic dreams because he has explored intel-lectual heights and depths with Settembrini and Naphta and because he has known the spectrum of humankind and human endeavor.

However, he who knows humankind, and the vitality of human-kind, also knows death. Such a concept is not intuitively new to Castorp, who learned the language and the moods of death before he had truly begun to appreciate life. All interest in disease and death is merely another means of expressing interest in life. In confessing that he has learned much during his Berghof sojourn about the human condition and about himself, Castorp realizes and admits his sympathy with those children of the sun in his dream who were "so sweetly courteous to each other, in silent recognition of that horror" (495) and not with Settembrini or Naphta. And yet, with respect to the development of his intellectual vitality and his quest for timelessness Castorp knows that he is indebted to both, and especially to Settembrini, for encour-agement and inspiration, whether positive or negative.

Castorp asserts the existential vitality of his position "between reck-lessness and reason . . . between mystic community and windy indi-vidualism" (496). Castorp states that he has made a dream poem of humanity—he wishes goodness and love of humankind to triumph over death, for love is stronger than death. The epiphanic moment of "Snow" culminates in the following assertion: "For the sake of goodness and love, man shall let death have no sovereignty over his thoughts" (496–97). With this realization Castorp awakes—he has reached his goal of supreme awareness and of an awareness of a transcendent power.

Berendsohn interprets the significance of Castorp's experience in "Snow" as follows:

> On awakening (from the dreams of a Grecian landscape) Castorp understands that he has escaped death once again. He draws a lesson from this dream vision which has shown him where mankind comes from and whither it strives. One must know about the abysses of the human soul and understand them—those abysses of cruelty, sickness, death, passion, and sin—otherwise one knows nothing of life. (75)

For the sake of goodness and love one should not let death have do-minion over one's thoughts. This experience of the imminence of death encourages Castorp to rejuvenate his devotion to life and perhaps initiates or precipitates his own ultimate demise. Castorp's experi-ence in the profound isolation of the snow represents an attempt to reconcile "kairos" and "aion," or even to unify "kairos" and "aion" in an emotionally heightened and intellectually intensified vision. The experience of such a vision implies Castorp's capacity to achieve a sense of timelessness.

In the discussion between Naphta and Settembrini about the Jesuits and the Freemasons Naphta makes an interesting point about alchemy, agreeing with Castorp that it meant transmuting into gold, and saying that it also represented purification, refinement, metamorphosis, transubstantiation into a higher state. Naphta claims that the primary symbol of alchemistic transmutation was the sepulchre: "Yes, the place of corruption. It comprehends all hermetics, all alchemy, it is nothing else than the receptacle, the well-guarded crystal retort wherein the material is compressed to its final transformation and purification" (511).

Castorp says that the word "hermetics" sounds like the use of magic and conjures up various vague and extended associations. For example, it reminds him of the conserve jars which his housekeeper in Hamburg keeps in the larder. For what is conserved is withdrawn from the effects of time—it is hermetically sealed from time. The conserve jars stand on the shelf shut away from time. Such a notion of alchemistic transmutation applies directly and effectively to the Berghof world. For Castorp has attempted, in his quest for timelessness, to attain a sense of being hermetically sealed, a sense of hermetic concealment from time, and to achieve a transformation of the self through the alchemistically vital aura of the Berghof.

What Naphta says about the importance of death in initiation ceremonies applies convincingly to the notion of Castorp's initiation into the hermetically isolated and sealed Berghof ambience. Naphta asserts that the grave, the sepulchre, has always been the emblem of initiation into the society and that the neophyte desiring admission to the mysteries must show exceptional courage in the face of their terrors. The grave is the abiding symbol of the Berghof, for so many of its residents become intimately linked with it and represented by it. Castorp enters the Berghof world as a neophyte with significant potential because of his early encounters with death. Unlike most of the other Berghof residents, Castorp experiences this sanatorium world on a higher intellectual and spiritual level, especially through the pedagogical efforts of Settembrini. Castorp, perhaps because he entered the Berghof world as an official outsider, as a guest of his cousin, experiences and participates in the sanatorium aura more intensely and intensively than others, especially when he finally becomes a patient. Castorp, a grail-seeker, a seeker after a sense of timelessness, chooses the path of mysteries and purification, the path of knowledge and self-liberating wisdom, the wisdom that liberates from the constraints of mortality and time.

Settembrini attempts to dissuade Castorp from his pious reverence for death. Settembrini believes that death is merely the end of a process of organic growth and decline—he shares the humanistic aversion to death which allows the physical seemingly to overcome the spiritual. Settembrini argues that the only appropriate way to think of death is as part of life, for death is only worthy of homage as the cradle of life, as the womb of palingenesis. Naphta counters with the important argument that without death there would never have been architecture, painting, sculpture, music, poetry, or any other art.

Both Thomas Mann and the American painter Frederic Church offer intense threshold moments at the interface of light and darkness, life and death. Church's *Mt. Ktaadn* (1853), *Twilight in the Wilderness* (1860), *Landscape, Sunset* (1850), and *Cotopaxi* (1863) signify the spirit of Hans Castorp's experience on the magic mountain. These paintings, especially the first three, show a mountain in the distance touched by the last light of the sunset, a mountain suffused with the final light of day before the inevitable emergence of night. Such a threshold experience is analogous to the epiphanic quality of Hans Castorp's emotional and intellectual experience on the magic mountain. For a prolonged moment (an epiphany of seeming timelessness which has the duration of seven years) comparable to Fitzgerald's "transitory enchanted moment" Castorp experiences the emotional and intellectual radiance and vitality which is ultimately diffused and diminished with the coming of the war.

There is also a similarity between Mann's magic mountain and Thomas Cole's *Schroon Mountain* (1838). In his essay "Church and Luminism: Light for America's Elect" David Huntington describes Cole's painting as follows:

> In the foreground, all is portrayed as struggle, strife, and suffering. Forms are blasted; colors are fiery. . . . To the poet-painter Thomas Cole this readymade natural drama preferred release from 'this vale of tears,' which it is man's sad fate to endure throughout his fleshly existence. . . . Here, nature for a moment might solace the individual pursuing his lonely pilgrimage through a sinful world. (164)

Hans Castorp leaves the flatland world of struggle, strife, and suffering to experience for a prolonged transitory enchanted moment on the magic mountain a release from this vale of tears. Ultimately, at the end of the novel he chooses to return to his lonely pilgrimage through 'the sinful world' of destruction and war—unfortunately, his attempt to influence such a world positively is short-lived.

It is significant that this chapter, chapter six, which has spoken of the importance of death imagery to an ambience of alchemistic transformation, ends with the death and burial of Castorp's cousin, Joachim Ziemssen. In the final paragraph of the chapter Mann emphasizes the lonely height on which his protagonist stands. Castorp seems to exist now forever at a distance, physically, intellectually, emotionally, and spiritually from the world of everyday reality down below. Yet it is perhaps not as negative an isolation as Settembrini would suggest— rather, it is an isolation of transformational possibilities, of transcendent vitality, of a sense of timelessness seemingly sanctified by alchemistic purification.

Chapter seven, the final chapter of the novel, begins with reflections on time. Mann declares the absurdity of narrating time for its own sake. Instead one must speak of narration filling up the time, as music does. Time is the medium of narration, as it is the medium of life: "both are inextricably bound up with it, as inextricably as are bodies in space" (541). Music and narration are alike because they present themselves as a flowing, as a succession in time.

Mann also distinguishes between the aspect of time in music and narration. For the time element in music is single, pouring itself into and enhancing a section of mortal time. However, a narrative must have two kinds of time—first, like music, its own actual time, and second, the time of its content. Mann proceeds to say that a narrative which concerns itself with the events of five minutes may, "by extraordinary conscientiousness in the telling, take up a thousand times five minutes" (542). On the other hand, the contentual time of a story can shrink its actual time out of all measure. In such an instance the story practices a hermetic magic, creating a distortion or transformation of temporal perspective which may offer a sense of timelessness.

Mann states that if Castorp had had to answer questions about specific dates and durations with respect to his experiences of the Berghof world, he would not have been able to do so. Mann makes an effective analogy between Castorp's inability to answer such specific questions about time and his incapacity to answer Settembrini's question, many evenings ago, about his age.

While Castorp agrees with the departed Joachim's point that the confusion of the seasons made the perception and conception of time chaotic, he shows already at the beginning of his Berghof stay an inclination to dabble in the mysterious and uncanny. Mann speaks of a giddiness which Castorp experiences, which made him prone to link "now" and "then" in a timeless eternity. Castorp appears to try to counter his inclination towards an experience of timeless eternity by watching time flow, observing the second-hand of his watch intensely "to cling to and prolong the passing moments" (545).

In the section "By the Ocean of Time," as previously in the novel, the image of the ocean is evoked to suggest eternity. The snowy wastes of the alpine landscape remind him of his native landscape of broad ocean dunes. In such an environment one may achieve a sense of timelessness: "You walk and walk—never will you come home at the right time, for you are of time, and time is vanished" (546). Participating emotionally and spiritually in the expansiveness of the ocean or the snowy landscape is an essential dimension of the experience of timelessness. Mann describes salient qualities of the shore and ocean which reinforce a sense of timelessness: "The dull, pervasive, sonorous roar closes our ears against all the sounds of the world. O deep content, O wilful bliss of sheer forgetfulness! Let us shut our eyes, safe in eternity" (547).

The section "By the Ocean of Time" ends with an ambivalent undertone. On the one hand, Mann asserts, in the spirit of Settembrini and in honor of Joachim, the fundamental importance of duty, of the law of life. The final sentence of the section, however, raises the question whether Castorp's quest for metaphysical solace and timelessness is not strengthened by his realization that Joachim's zeal for conformity, for the "flatland" approach to life, for a philosophy of life which was dependent upon "flatland" conceptions of time, had brought him to his fatal end. Though Mann speaks of Castorp's traffic with eternity as somewhat baleful, does he not ultimately support Castorp's quest for a sense of timelessness which fulfills the promise of literature in its striving for understanding, forgiveness, and love?

The appearance of the gramophone at the Berghof causes considerable excitement. Castorp feels instinctively that he should be in charge of it: "he was filled with the surest foreknowledge of a new passion, a new enchantment, a new burden of love" (639). By himself in the night Castorp plays several records all of which have a romantic undertone. With respect to one song in particular, the one about the linden-tree, Castorp feels an intimate emotional participation. Mann describes Castorp's feeling as a conception of the spirit aware of its own significance and yet reaching beyond itself to express a larger world of feeling and sentiment. Such a feeling is analogous in intensity and scope to the transformation of Beethoven's personal experience of despair in the Funeral March of the "Eroica" into a representation of a broader and more general human experience.

Mann asserts that Castorp, after years of hermetic-pedagogic discipline, of ascent from one stage of being to another, has reached a point where he is conscious of the meaningfulness of his love and the object of it. In declaring the importance and necessity of the feeling of soul-enchantment which such music inspires, despite the suggestion of Settembrini that it may bear sinister fruit, Mann anticipates the claim of Jean-Paul Sartre that by pursuing transcendent aims man is able to exist. Of the powerful influence of this soul-enchantment on his protagonist Mann writes that Castorp's thoughts, or rather his prophetic half-thoughts soared higher than his understanding and were alchemistically enhanced.

The emotional, psychological, spiritual power of this soul-enchantment is so strong, says Mann, that kingdoms may be founded on it, or the soul-enchantment might possess the life of an individual so that such an individual may die for it in self-conquest or because of enchantment. But he who dies for it does so as an innovator, a harbinger of the new world of love which shall spread perhaps as widely as Settembrini's conviction in progress and rational enlightenment. Yet, is it proper to speak of death in the existential context of one who has embarked, though not entirely of his own accord, on a quest for timelessness? Is the fulfillment of the soul-enchantment not compatible with the attainment of the grail, with the inspirational completion of the quest for timelessness? Is self-conquest in the spirit of this transcendent love not analogous to the achievement of at least a vital semblance of timelessness? Is the refreshment of the spirit, which occurs in the experience of transcendent musical vitality, not synonymous with an enchanted moment, as transitory as it may outwardly seem to be, of timelessness?

The highly questionable seance and the passionately primitive duel between Settembrini and Naphta challenge and perhaps even undermine the aura of timeless serenity which Castorp has come to associate with the sanatorium, an aura which signifies the spiritual essence of the experience of timelessness. When Settembrini accuses Naphta of having an infamous way of dealing with youth, Naphta challenges him to a duel to defend his honor and principles.

At the duel Settembrini says he will not kill and fires into the air. Naphta is disturbed by this response and shoots himself in the head. Perhaps Naphta can endure his quest for absolute truth no longer. He has perhaps devoted himself so assiduously to the ideal and to ideal truths that when he is confronted by reality, when reality in the form of a duel demands that he fulfill certain conventions, he cannot. Or perhaps Naphta's shooting of himself and not Settembrini signifies his underlying humanistic outlook, namely, that he could not kill another human being. The sudden removal of Naphta as an intellectual presence on the magic mountain and from intellectual intercourse with Settembrini and Castorp also undermines the seemingly timeless ambience. For timelessness can be most effectively preserved without such dramatic changes. The duel foreshadows the ending of the novel by introducing the theme of death in conjunction with the theme of personal and social responsibility.

In the final section of the novel, entitled "The Thunder-Bolt," Mann writes that Castorp is treated ultimately "like the scholar in the particularly happy state of never being asked any more, of never having a task, of being left to sit, . . . and no one troubles about him further— an orgiastic kind of freedom" (706).

Through this passage and other similar ones Mann seems to corroborate Castorp's achievement of timelessness. The death of old Consul Tienappel, Hans' great-uncle and foster-father, strengthened Castorp's sense of freedom from the world down below, from flatland concerns and values. Castorp's increasing lack of interest in the passage of time is described: "Thus he did honor to his abiding-everlasting, his walk by the ocean of time, the hermetic enchantment to which he had proved so extraordinarily susceptible that it had become the fundamental adventure of his life" (708).

Then, suddenly, the thunder-peal occurs, as primitive and abrupt and potentially destructive as the duel between Naphta and Settembrini; a thunder-peal which made the foundation of the earth shake and even startled the "seven-sleeper" Castorp. He who had not shown an interest in Settembrini's attempt to make him critically aware of current world events, he who had occupied himself with "the subjective shadows of things," now sat at Settembrini's bedside to listen to his comments on the state of Europe. Moreover, the newspapers fulfilled the potential of the Word to awaken and stimulate, and aroused Castorp, who feels that he has been "freed" from his "enchantment" by the operation of external powers. Mann captures the metaphysical tension evoked by the thunder-peal in a letter to Paul Amann in which he suggests that the novel entails a Rip Van Winkle-like experience which will end in the outbreak of war. Mann reinforces this tension in describing the spirit of the work as humorous-nihilistic with a tendency towards a sympathy with death.

Not only does Mann describe Castorp as now being freed from enchantment—he also suggests that his protagonist has "sinned" by participating so fully and willingly in the timeless enchantment. Has Hans Castorp, "whose tiny destiny fainted to nothing in the face of the general," sinned by devoting himself to his quest for timelessness? Or has he not rather assumed a mythological vitality, has he not instead become a symbolic representative of the human condition, the collective unconscious, in his quest for timelessness? Does he not carry the burden, in the heroic tradition of Atlas-like figures, in his own quest for timelessness of a collective, a communal quest for timelessness? Does not Thomas Mann underestimate the emotional and intellectual vitality of his protagonist? Has not Castorp, through his own self-conquest, his intellectual exchanges with Settembrini and Naphta, his intellectual and spiritual progress, and his transcendent striving proven that he is no longer life's erring and delicate child?

Castorp does leave the Berghof world out of a vague sense of social responsibility and duty to his country. One might also argue, as do Horst S. and Ingrid G. Daemmrich in *Spirals and Circles*, that "the narrator is compelled to abandon Castorp once the hermetic spell of the atmosphere is broken by the clash of societies which collectively failed to gain historical awareness" (2: 8). Or perhaps the primary reason for Castorp's departure is that his sense of timelessness has been disrupted and undermined, for the Berghof no longer offers a serene sanctuary from the world, or at least Castorp is lead, by external factors, to believe that it does not.

Is the intense awareness of this disruption of a sense of timelessness not as strong for Castorp as it is for Robert Faehmel in Heinrich Böll's *Billiards at Half-Past Nine?* Whereas Faehmel's sense of timelessness, articulated as an enchanted moment in the realistically etherial aura of the Prinz Heinrich billiard room, is agitated permanently by a figure from the past—the return of Schrella—Castorp's sense of timeless enchantment is eradicated by the remembrance of the past, of Joachim's dream, and by a renewed awareness of the exigencies of the present. Moreover, Castorp has a silent, unconscious yearning for solemnity and death—and he feels that he might function as a substitute for Joachim on the flatland battleground. In attempting to fulfill Joachim's dream Castorp feels that he is part of an experience larger than himself—in serving his country and his cousin's memory Castorp strives to realize and sustain a sense of social and personal responsibility.

Does not Castorp reveal himself as an existential humanist, fulfilling the intellectual and social challenge of Jean-Paul Sartre in *Existentialism and Humanism?* Sartre writes: "Man is all the time outside of himself: it is in projecting and losing himself beyond himself that he makes man to exist; and, on the other hand, it is by pursuing transcendent aims that he himself is able to exist" (59). While Castorp certainly shows a strong capacity for self-surpassing—a capacity which he has consciously as well as unconsciously nurtured on the magic mountain—he has not fully and consciously realized, as Sartre would say of the existential humanist, that he is himself the heart and center of his transcendence. In entering the military conflict Castorp perhaps challenges his eternally transcendent aims and undermines the possibility of considering himself the heart and center of his own transcendence.

Sartre describes existential humanism as the relation of transcendence as constitutive of man with subjectivity:

> This is humanism; because we remind man that there is no legislator but himself; that he himself, thus abandoned, must decide for himself; also because we show that it is not by turning back upon himself, but always by seeking beyond himself, an aim which is one of liberation or of some particular realization, that man can realize himself as truly human. (59)

Castorp, once the timeless enchantment of the Magic Mountain is broken, acts upon his inalienably vital conviction that there is no legislator but himself and affirms his intuitive existential humanism by seeking beyond himself in a potentially self-destructive gesture of dynamic social responsibility.

Ultimately, the Berghof dream becomes the agony and misery of the flatland war, where Castorp staggers in the tumult, the rain, the dusk, and finally vanishes out of the author's sight. In saying farewell to his protagonist, Mann claims that his tale was a hermetic one. He says he told the tale for its own sake—nevertheless, it was Hans Castorp's tale, because he developed into a distinctively sensitive, thoughtful, and significant protagonist.

The Magic Mountain, despite the fact that its final scenario involves death, destruction, and war, ends with a seemingly optimistic, provisionally affirmative undertone: "Out of this universal feast of death, out of this extremity of fever, kindling the rain-washed evening sky to

a fiery glow, may it be that Love one day shall mount?" (716). Might
this question not apply equally well to both the war and the Berghof
environment which signifies a symbolic feast of death? Might one not
ask whether Castorp's expression of Love, his self-sacrificial, heroic
gesture is a manifestation of his quest for timelessness, for the serene
timelessness and timeless vitality of the human spirit?

Conclusion

In his introduction to James Thomson's *The Seasons* James Sambrook describes the extremes of nature and the consequences for Thomson's persona while stating that "the spectacle of uncontrolled power in nature evokes salutary fear and reverential awe which turn the mind towards God" (xviii). Sambrook proceeds to suggest that "astronomical and geographical excursions . . . arouse that pleasure which the imagination found in the vastness of the natural world" (xviii). The theme of imaginative development in the spaciousness of the natural world, whether or not it is connected to an awareness of the divine, is crucial to the magic mountain experiences of Wordsworth, Arnold, Hilton, and Mann.

In the expansiveness of the universe the persona experiences a vital sense of the development of his imaginative capacity and perhaps even finds evidence of a divine presence. In "Spectator 489," for example, Addison wrote that the imagination stimulates the understanding and "by the Greatness of the sensible Object produces in it the Idea of a Being who is neither circumscribed by Time nor Space" (Sambrook xix). Such a being is the mind that feeds upon infinity, the majestic intellect of Wordsworth's *The Prelude*.

In "Spectator 420" Addison offers another sense of infinity which is less terrestrial than astronomical. After describing the pleasing sensation which an observation of the earth produces, Addison writes:

> If, after this, we contemplate those wild fields of ether, that reach in height as far as from Saturn to the fixed stars, and run abroad almost to an infinitude, our imagination finds its capacity filled with so immense a prospect, and puts itself upon the stretch to comprehend it. (No. 420, 2 July 1712)

The emphasis on the development of the imagination in the spaciousness of nature is reaffirmed in Thomas Burnet's *The Theory of the Earth* (1684–90) which stresses the inspirational quality of the great objects of nature:

> The greatest objects of Nature are . . . the most pleasing to behold; and next to the great Concave of the Heavens, and those boundless Regions where the Stars inhabit, there is nothing that I look upon with more pleasure than the wide Sea and the Mountains of the Earth. There is something august and stately in the Air of these things that inspires the mind with great thoughts and passions. (Book 1, chap. xi)

Burnet's world-view is in keeping with the Newtonian conception of the universe which believed that God was present in the universe to preserve its order and that God was the controlling force in infinite space. Wordsworth, though he believes in a divine presence in nature (a belief which changes, for example, from the pantheism of 1798–99 to the notion of a mind-divine continuum in 1804–05), is interested in *The Prelude* in asserting the importance of the dynamically imaginative creative persona in the diastolic aura of nature.

These eighteenth-century perspectives on the imagination culminate in Coleridge's sense of the imaginative power. In *Biographia Literaria* Coleridge describes the primary imagination as the living power and primary agent of all human perception. Moreover, it is a repetition in the finite mind of God's act of creation. The secondary imagination is an echo of the primary, "co-existing with the conscious will" (Perkins 452). In the moment of imaginative power when the mortal mind perceives its relation to God, it also transcends the limits of the physical self and becomes quasi-divine in its creativity.

It is such a quasi-divine creativity which enables the Wordsworthian self to achieve a diastolic sense of space and time. J. Wordsworth, M. Jaye, and others address the issue of the imagination in the age of English Romanticism, stressing the importance of inner voices for the Wordsworth of *The Prelude*:

> The voices mounting through the mist are—or can be seen as being—internal. They combine to form that experience which the poet, in a supreme Romantic intuition, suggests may be either 'the sense of God' or the sense of an autonomous power deep within the self. (197)

G. Poulet says in *Studies in Human Time* that the romantic tries to envelop his lifelong consciousness in the sphere of the present moment. It is a question of giving the moment a profundity, an infinity of duration. There is, for example, the romanticism of experienced continuity—the mind unifies in a moving line the diverse temporal elements of an individual existence. Poulet says that for the nineteenth century human time and cosmic time are continuous. The time of inward duration and clock time are fused in a single continuity. The personae in the works of Wordsworth, Arnold, Hilton, and Mann all try to achieve such a dynamic sense of continuity.

As in Tennyson's *In Memoriam* (where the experience of reading Hallam's letters leads Tennyson to a mystical revelation) the "past briefly recovered leads to a vision of that which is, a state of absolute being beyond the realm of death, chance, and time" (Buckley 111), so in Wordsworth's "Immortality Ode" and *The Prelude* the mortal limit of the self is freed in a vital "spot of time." This Wordsworthian "spot of time" is similar in focus and intensity to Walter Pater's moment of "quickened, multiplied consciousness" as well as to James Joyce's epiphany in its emphasis on a sudden spiritual manifestation, a revelation that brings a sense of timeless harmony.

Arnold's persona in "Stanzas from the Grande Chartreuse" as well as the protagonists in Hilton's *Lost Horizon* and Mann's *The Magic Mountain* achieve such a sense of timeless harmony as well the vitality of which is intimately linked to an experience of the spaciousness or spatial expansiveness of nature.

Poulet's moment of experienced continuity is analogous to Buckley's "intense and privileged moment" in which "art, especially poetry, might suggest that time itself, as man reckons it, was after all man's own invention, a device for dividing eternity into negotiable parts" (153). One might think of Tennyson's persona in "The Ancient Sage" speaking of breaking the Eternal Now into "Thens" and "Whens." Buckley concludes his discussion of the importance of the intense and privileged moment by saying that "in restoring even briefly a sense of integration, unity, and design, art could reduce to harmless illusion the terror of time" (153).

In the essay "Romantic Space: Topo-analysis and Subjectivity in *The Prelude*" Philip Shaw suggests that for Coleridge and for Wordsworth "mental space has far more to do with the philosophy of transcendence than with the Faery land of medieval romance" (71). Shaw says of the relation between landscape and imagination:

> In *The Prelude* whenever social space threatens to overwhelm the self, to return it to the body, as in Revolutionary France, the 'power of landscape' intervenes as a kind of supplement . . . to relegate social space to the background and to reaffirm the mental space of the imagination. (80)

Shaw argues later that by the end of the text what has been restored is not "the real landscape—not the space of daily life and practical relations" (93) but rather "the false, aesthetic landscape of pastoralism" (93). To Shaw, "Wordsworth resists historical space to fashion himself in the artifice of eternity" (93).

What Shaw perhaps misinterprets in his argument is Wordsworth's understanding of and sensitivity towards space. Wordsworth does show a conspicuously historical sense of space in his chapters in *The Prelude* on his experience in France. In the other chapters, where the emphasis is less overtly "historical," Wordsworth is concerned with personal history, with a portrayal of the emotional, intellectual, and spiritual dimensions of the creative self in the context of Nature. Through the present, or presence, of Nature the poetic persona finds and preserves his own sense of meaning and purpose in life, his own sense of personal history.

One might even say that through his awareness that the majestic intellect will ultimately shape an existential condition when "Time shall be no more" (14.111), the poet creates his own sense of history, a history at least as powerful and subjective and certainly more visionary than the more overtly historical approach. For the majestic intellect, time and history are ultimately subsumed in space and nature—in the spaciousness of nature the poetic persona achieves an expansive sense of space and time.

The last two stanzas of the "Immortality Ode" stress the significance of the faith that looks through death in conjunction with an extraordinary emotional vitality. This same combination of features is essential to the magic mountain experience of *The Prelude*. In Book 14 Wordsworth's persona asserts the importance of the majestic intellect, the mind that feeds upon infinity which has the power to converse with the spiritual world and with past, present, and future generations of humankind. Such a mind is most vital when it signifies the "feeling intellect."

Such a feeling, majestic intellect is analogous to the minds of Arnold's persona in "Stanzas from the Grande Chartreuse," of Conway in *Lost Horizon*, and of Castorp in *The Magic Mountain*. One might even argue that the intellects of these characters are emanations or manifestations of the majestic intellect of Wordsworth's *The Prelude*.

As the "Snow" episode of Mann's *The Magic Mountain*, so the vision of Wordsworth's persona in Book 14 culminates in an effusion of light. The mind that the persona describes is a mind at the threshold of life and death:

There I beheld the emblem of a mind
That feeds upon infinity, that broods
Over the dark abyss, intent to hear
Its voices issuing forth to silent light
In one continuous stream. (14.70–74)

Such a mind at the interface of infinity and mortality can achieve a sense of spaciousness and timelessness. Whereas Hilton's protagonist in *Lost Horizon* only envisions living in an existential condition which slows down the process of time, Wordsworth's persona actually asserts his conviction in the prospect of an atemporal or timeless existence. Thomas Mann's protagonist, though he creates a "dream-poem" about humanity which culminates in his assertion that love should triumph over death, ultimately realizes and acknowledges the mortality of human existence.

Arnold's persona in "Stanzas from the Grande Chartreuse," perhaps the defining persona in the quest for an inner serenity in harmony with a subtly vital spatiality and temporality, ends up in a secluded place away from the world of evanescence. This sense of distance from such a world is affirmed in various paintings and watercolors from the late eighteenth century to the mid-nineteenth century. The rugged isolation of the Grande Chartreuse is depicted in such works as J. M. W. Turner's *Llanthony Abbey* (1834) and *Mer de Glace, Chamonix, with Blair's Hut* (1806) and J. R. Cozens' *Pays de Valais* (1780). Cozens' *Pays de Valais* and Turner's *Mer de Glace* present an emotionally and spiritually vital landscape that is physically differentiated from the world of everyday mortality. The sublime serenity of Cozens' *Pays de Valais* as well as his *In the Canton of Unterwalden* (1780) contrasts with the natural energy and dynamic light of some of Turner's mountain landscapes.

Cozens' *In the Canton of Unterwalden* signifies especially effectively the aura of the Grande Chartreuse which Matthew Arnold's persona experiences in "Stanzas from the Grande Chartreuse." The etherial tranquillity of this watercolor, which Cozens made on his first tour of Switzerland and Italy with Payne Knight, affirms the emotional, spiritual vitality of this world apart from everyday mortality. The sense of isolated seclusion, of tranquil differentiation from the vicissitudes of everyday mortality, is also seen in Turner's *Llanthony Abbey* (1794). In this work, the monastery, though a physical ruin, has an emotional and spiritual integrity and life all its own, symbolic of the isolated splendor of the Grande Chartreuse monastery which Arnold's persona experiences. Although the mortal flux of the secular world al-

most impinges upon the monastery, it is protected and preserved by a
sense of etherial tranquillity and of serene wisdom which not only
infuses the Grande Chartreuse with a dynamically hermetic spiritual
power but which also radiates from the persona with a revitalizing
energy at least as cyclically powerful as the "accents of the eternal
tongue" (125–26) playing perpetually through the pine branches in
"Stanzas in Memory of the Author of 'Obermann'."

On the magic mountain Arnold's persona realizes the hermetic,
limiting nature of time and space. For Arnold the mountain is no longer
(as it was for Wordsworth) a place of potential, of possibilities for
personal and cultural growth, but rather a space for the dissolution or
sublimation of the self. The closing stanza (lines 205–10) of "Stanzas
from the Grande Chartreuse" affirms the hermetic nature of time and
space experienced by the persona:

> Fenced early in this cloistral round
> Of reverie, of shade, of prayer,
> How should we grow in other ground?
> How can we flower in foreign air?
> —Pass, banners, pass, and bugles, cease,
> And leave our desert to its peace!

The sense of being in a threshold realm of life and death is crucial
to the magic mountain experiences of the protagonists in Wordsworth,
Arnold, Hilton, and Mann. Only in the twilight realm (which Nietzsche
describes as the domain of music), the threshold ambience, of the
magic mountain at the interface of life and death can Castorp achieve
an intellectual and spiritual awakening. Castorp's participation in this
threshold realm, which is initially more unconscious and intuitive than
conscious, leads to an expansiveness of self (culminating in a sense of
the expansiveness of space and time) in which he gives himself emotionally and intellectually to the sublimity of the aura of death.

Erich Heller in *Thomas Mann: The Ironic German* asserts that the
narrative tension in the novel reinforces the threshold nature of the
experience of Castorp in the "Snow" section:

> The story of *The Magic Mountain* is, as it were, told twice: once as a series
> of incidents and experiences, and then again as a series of intimations con-
> veyed through the very shape of the work. The arrangement of the two is not
> smoothly harmonious, but ironical and contrapuntal, like the two parts . . . of
> the dream Hans Castorp has in the snow, the 'dream poem of humanity.' (29)

In discussing threshold figures in *The Inner Reaches of Outer Space* Joseph Campbell writes that such figures at the threshold of the passage from time to eternity are simultaneously of two worlds, "temporal in the human appeal of their pictured denotations, while by connotation opening to eternity" (69). Only those individuals who show a capacity to perceive the infinite and to conceive of eternity and who reveal themselves as threshold-figures, as figures at the interface, literally or symbolically, of time and infinity can develop an effective strategy of confronting mortality and the flux of time.

Campbell's subsequent analysis of Albrecht Dürer's woodcuts of scenes of the Crucifixion is especially relevant to the narrative experiences of the magic mountain protagonists in Wordsworth, Arnold, Hilton, and Mann. Campbell stresses a formal and thematic parallel between Dürer's Crucifixion woodcuts and Tibetan processional banners both of which contain disks of the sun and the moon in the upper left and right corners. These images are references to the moment "of the moon rising full on its fifteenth night, confronting with equal radiance the sun setting at that moment on the opposite horizon: the moon not quenched in solar light, but fully illuminated, self-equaling" (70).

Campbell proceeds to interpret the significance of these threshold images in greater detail:

> For these are threshold forms at the interface of time and eternity. Read in one direction, they symbolize the passage of the light of consciousness from engagement in the field of birth and death to identification with an immortal source, 'which neither is born, nor does it ever die; nor, having once been will it cease to be. Unborn, eternal, perpetual and primeval, it is not slain when the body is slain.' (*Bhagavad Gita* 2:20) (70)

Such a threshold figure is Hilton's Conway, who not only fulfilled the Mahayana Buddhist ideal of the Bodhisattva in returning from Shangri-La to the suffering world, at least temporarily, to "teach" (to spread the aesthetic, intellectual, and spiritual gospel of Shangri-La) but also, in being chosen by the High Lama, affirms his already inner-generated ascension to the level of the eternal and perpetual. Such a threshold figure is also Wordsworth's majestic intellect who not only has a vital humanitarian sympathy with the world but also envisions the end of time.

Of the images read in the other direction Campbell writes:

The figures represent . . . the willing participation in the sorrows of space-
time of one who, though in the knowledge of himself as of the nature of
immortal bliss, yet voluntarily, as an avatar (Sanskrit 'avatara,' meaning 'he
passes across or over') joyfully engages in the fragmentation of life in Time.
(72)

Such a threshold figure is Hans Castorp who in his magic mountain
sojourn has achieved a sense of the timeless self and a sense of the
immortal bliss of timelessness—ultimately, however, he sacrifices himself for the cause of humankind.

The quest for an understanding of time and space is essential to
the magic mountain experiences of the personae and protagonists
discussed above. Yet, in achieving a prolonged sense or temporary
semblance of the spatial and/or temporal expansiveness of the self,
these individuals are inspired to develop and strengthen their humanitarian vitality and to experience their individual self as a Universal
Self.

Schopenhauer in his essay "On the Foundation of Morality" describes such an experience of the universal self as Other and inner
self: "This presupposes that I have to some extent identified myself
with the other and therewith removed for the moment the barrier
between the 'I' and the 'Not-I.' Only then can the other's situation, his
want, his need, become mine" (Campbell 112). The other is not perceived as different from the 'I'; rather, the 'I' exists in a dynamic condition of emotional, spiritual, and intellectual unity with the other as
well as with the inner self.

Even though the world of mortality may not understand or appreciate the creative and humanitarian vitality of the personae and protagonists in Wordsworth, Arnold, Hilton, and Mann as sensitively as it
should, these individuals realize that their artistic vision will always be
preserved as long as they sustain their emotional and spiritual connection with nature and with the Universal Self, as long as they participate in the motion and the spirit of the

> sense sublime
> Of something far more deeply interfused
> Whose dwelling is the light of setting suns,
> And the round ocean and the living air,
> And the blue sky, and in the mind of man.
> ("Tintern Abbey" 95–99)

Works Consulted

Introduction

Abrams, M. H. "Revolutionary Romanticism 1790–1990." *Wordsworth in Context*. Ed. Pauline Fletcher and John Murphy. Lewisburg: Bucknell UP, 1992. 19–34.

Arnold, Matthew. *Selected Poems and Prose*. Ed. Miriam Allott. London: J. M. Dent, 1978.

Baillie, John. *An Essay on the Sublime*. 1747. Los Angeles: The Augustan Society, 1953.

Beja, Morris. *Epiphany in the Modern Novel*. Seattle: U of Washington P, 1979.

Buckley, Jerome H. *The Triumph of Time*. Cambridge, Mass.: Harvard UP, 1966.

Burke, Edmund. *Philosophical Enquiry into the Origin of Our Ideas of the Sublime and the Beautiful*. London, 1757.

Gerard, Alexander. *An Essay on Taste*. 3rd ed. Edinburgh, 1780.

Gray, Thomas. *The Poems and Letters of Thomas Gray*. Ed. William Mason. London, 1820.

Hanley, Keith. "'A Poet's History': Wordsworth and Revolutionary Discourse." *Wordsworth in Context*. Ed. Pauline Fletcher and John Murphy. Lewisburg: Bucknell UP, 1992. 36–65.

Hazlitt, William. *The Spirit of the Age*. London, 1825.

Hilton, James. *Lost Horizon*. New York: William Morrow, 1934.

House, Humphry. "The Mood of Doubt." *Ideas and Beliefs of the Victorians*. New York: E. P. Dutton, 1966.

Knight, Richard Payne. *Analytical Inquiry into the Principles of Taste*. London, 1805.

Kroeber, Karl. *Romantic Landscape Vision: Constable and Wordsworth*. Madison: U of Wisconsin P, 1975.

Macartney, C. E. *Mountains and Mountain Men of the Bible*. New York: Abingdon-Cokesbury P.

Mann, Thomas. *The Magic Mountain*. Trans. H. Lowe-Porter. New York: Alfred A. Knopf, 1961.

Mill, John Stuart. *The Spirit of the Age*. Ed. Frederick A. von Hayek. Chicago: U of Chicago P, 1942.

Nicolson, Marjorie H. *Mountain Gloom and Mountain Glory*. Ithaca: Cornell UP, 1959.

Novak, Barbara. "On Defining Luminism." *American Light: The Luminist Movement*. Ed. John Wilmerding. Washington: National Gallery of Art, 1980.

Perkins, David, ed. *English Romantic Writers*. San Diego: Harcourt Brace, 1967.

Poulet, Georges. *Studies in Human Time*. Trans. Elliott Coleman. Baltimore: Johns Hopkins UP, 1956.

Priestly, Joseph. *A Course of Lectures on Oratory and Criticism*. London, 1777.

Schiller, Friedrich. *Essays*. Ed. Walter Hinderer and Daniel O. Dahlstrom. New York: Continuum.

Thompson, David, ed. and trans. *Petrarch*. New York: Harper & Row, 1971.

Tuveson, Ernst Lee. *The Imagination as a Means of Grace*. Berkeley: U of California P, 1960.

Williams, Raymond. *Culture and Society: 1780–1950*. New York: Columbia UP, 1960.

Wilton, Andrew. *Turner and the Sublime*. London: British Museum Publications, 1980.

Wlecke, Albert O. *Wordsworth and the Sublime.* Berkeley: U of Califomia P, 1973.

Wordsworth, William. *The Prelude* (1799, 1805, 1850). Ed. Jonathan Wordsworth, M. H. Abrams, and Stephan Gill. New York: W. W. Norton, 1979.

Chapter 1

Abrams, M. H. *The Mirror and the Lamp: Romantic Theory and the Critical Tradition.* New York: The Norton Library, 1958.

———. "Revolutionary Romanticism 1790–1990." *Wordsworth in Context.* Ed Pauline Fletcher and John Murphy. Lewisburg: Bucknell UP, 1992. 19–34.

Averill, James H. *Wordsworth and Human Suffering.* Ithaca: Cornell UP, 1980.

Baillie, John. *An Essay on the Sublime.* 1747. Los Angeles: The Augustan Society, 1953.

Baker, Jeffrey. *Time and Mind in Wordsworth's Poetry.* Detroit: Wayne State UP, 1980.

Bate, Jonathan. *Romantic Ecology: Wordsworth and the Environmental Tradition.* London: Routledge, 1991.

Beer, John. *Wordsworth in Time.* London: Faber, 1979.

Bloom, Harold. *The Visionary Company.* Garden City, N. Y.: Doubleday, 1961.

———, ed. and intro. *William Wordsworth's "The Prelude."* New York: Chelsea House, 1986.

Brooks, Cleanth. *The Well-Wrought Urn.* London: Dennis Dobson, 1968.

Butler, Marilyn. *Romantics, Rebels, and Reactionaries.* Oxford: Oxford UP, 1981.

Curran, Stuart. *Poetic Form and British Romanticism.* New York: Oxford UP, 1986.

Durrant, Geoffrey. *Wordsworth and the Great System.* Cambridge: Cambridge UP, 1986.

Fletcher, Pauline, and John Murphy, eds. *Wordsworth in Context*. Lewisburg: Bucknell UP, 1992.

Friedman, Michael H. *The Making of a Tory Humanist: William Wordsworth and the Idea of Community*. New York: Columbia UP, 1979.

Gerard, Alexander. *An Essay on Taste*. 3rd ed. Edinburgh, 1780.

Gill, Stephen. *William Wordsworth: A Life*. Oxford: Clarendon P, 1989.

Gilpin, George H., ed. *Critical Essays on William Wordsworth*. Boston: G. K. Hall, 1990.

Hanley, Keith. "'A Poet's History': Wordsworth and Revolutionary Discourse." *Wordsworth in Context*. Ed. Pauline Fletcher and John Murphy. Lewisburg: Bucknell UP, 1992. 35–65.

Hartman, Geoffrey. "The Romance of Nature and the Negative Way." *William Wordsworth's "The Prelude."* Ed. Harold Bloom. New York: Chelsea House, 1986. 57–75.

———. *The Unremarkable Wordsworth*. Minneapolis: UP of Minnesota, 1987.

———. *Wordsworth's Poetry, 1787–1814*. New Haven: Yale UP, 1964.

Hazlitt, William. *The Spirit of the Age*. London, 1825.

Heffernan, James A. W. *The ReCreation of Landscape: A Study of Wordsworth, Coleridge, Constable, and Turner*. Hanover, New Hampshire: UP of New England, 1984.

Jacobus, Mary. "Apostrophe and Lyric Voice in *The Prelude*." *William Wordsworth's "The Prelude."* Ed. Harold Bloom. New York: Chelsea House, 1986. 145–59.

Johnson, Karl R. *The Written Spirit: Thematic and Rhetorical Structure in Wordsworth's "The Prelude."* Salzburg: Salzburg Studies in English, 1978.

Johnston, Kenneth R., and Gene W. Ruoff, eds. *The Age of William Wordsworth: Critical Essays on the Romantic Tradition*. New Brunswick, N. J.: Rutgers UP, 1987.

Knight, Richard Payne. *Analytical Inquiry into the Principles of Taste.* London, 1805.

Kroeber, Karl. *Romantic Landscape Vision: Constable and Wordsworth.* Madison: U of Wisconsin P, 1975.

Langbaum, Robert. *The Mysteries of Identity.* Oxford: Oxford UP, 1979.

Lindenberger, Herbert. "The Structural Unit: 'Spots of Time.'" *William Wordsworth's "The Prelude."* Ed. Harold Bloom. New York: Chelsea House, 1986. 77–88.

Liu, Alan. *Wordsworth: The Sense of History.* Stanford: Stanford UP, 1989.

Mill, John Stuart. *The Spirit of the Age.* Ed. Frederick A. von Hayek. Chicago: U of Chicago P, 1942.

Nichols, Ashton. "The Revolutionary 'I': Wordsworth and the Politics of Self-Presentation." *Wordsworth in Context.* Ed. Pauline Fletcher and John Murphy. Lewisburg: Bucknell UP, 1992. 66–84.

Perkins, David, ed. *English Romantic Writers.* San Diego: Harcourt Brace, 1967.

Pirie, David. *William Wordsworth: The Poetry of Grandeur and of Tenderness.* London: Methuen, 1982.

Prickett, Stephen. *Coleridge and Wordsworth: The Poetry of Growth.* Cambridge: Cambridge UP, 1970.

Priestly, Joseph. *A Course of Lectures on Oratory and Criticism.* London, 1777.

Schiller, Friedrich. *Essays.* Ed. Walter Hinderer and Daniel O. Dahlstrom. New York: Continuum.

Simpson, David E. "The Spots of Time: Spaces for Refiguring." *William Wordsworth's "The Prelude."* Ed. Harold Bloom. New York: Chelsea House, 1986. 137–44.

Vendler, Helen. *"Tintern Abbey:* Two Assaults." *Wordsworth in Context.* Ed. Pauline Fletcher and John Murphy. Lewisburg: Bucknell UP, 1992. 173–90.

Ward, J. P. *Wordsworth's Language of Man*. Sussex: The Harvester P, 1984.

Welsford, Enid. *Salisbury Plain: A Study in the Development of Wordsworth's Mind and Art*. Oxford: Oxford UP, 1966.

Wesling, Donald. *Wordsworth and the Adequacy of Landscape*. London: Routledge & Kegan Paul, 1970.

Williams, Raymond. *Culture and Society: 1780–1950*. New York: Columbia UP, 1960.

Wlecke, Albert O. *Wordsworth and the Sublime*. Berkeley: U of California P, 1973.

Wordsworth, Jonathan. *The Borders of Vision*. Oxford: Clarendon P, 1982.

Wordsworth, William. *The Prelude* (1799, 1805, 1850). Ed. Jonathan Wordsworth, M. H. Abrams, and Stephen Gill. New York: W. W. Norton, 1979.

Chapter 2

Alexander, Edward. *Matthew Arnold, John Ruskin, and the Modern Temper*. Columbus: Ohio State UP, 1973.

Allott, Miriam, ed. and intro. *Matthew Arnold—Selected Poems and Prose*. London: J. M. Dent, 1978.

Anderson, Warren D. *Matthew Arnold and the Classical Tradition*. Ann Arbor: U of Michigan P, 1965.

Bloom, Harold, ed. *Matthew Arnold*. New York: Chelsea House, 1987.

Buckler, William E. *On the Poetry of Matthew Arnold: Essays in Critical Reconstruction*. New York: New York UP, 1982.

Burnham, Peter. "'Empedocles on Etna' and Matthew Arnold's Argument with History." *Arnoldian* 12.1 (1984): 1–21.

Bush, Douglas. *Matthew Arnold*. New York: Macmillan, 1971.

Carroll, Joseph. *The Cultural Theory of Matthew Arnold*. Berkeley: U of California P, 1982.

Gottfried, Leon. *Matthew Arnold and the Romantics*. London: Routledge & Kegan Paul, 1963.

Honan, Park. *Matthew Arnold: A Life*. New York: McGraw-Hill, 1981.

Houghton, Walter E., and G. Robert Stange. *Victorian Poetry and Poetics*. Boston: Houghton Mifflin, 1968.

House, Humphry. "The Mood of Doubt." *Ideas and Beliefs of the Victorians*. New York: E. P. Dutton, 1966.

Machann, Clinton, and Forrest D. Burt, eds. *Matthew Arnold in His Time and Ours: Centenary Essays*. Charlottesville: UP of Virginia, 1988.

Mayer, Elizabeth, and Marianne Moore, trans. *Stones of Many Colors*. New York: Pantheon, 1965.

Neiman, Fraser. *Matthew Arnold*. New York: Twayne, 1968.

Pratt, Linda R. "Matthew Arnold and the Modernist Image." *Matthew Arnold in His Time and Ours: Centenary Essays*. Ed. Clinton Machann and Forrest D. Burt. Charlottesville: UP of Virginia, 1988.

Roberts, Ruth. *Arnold and God*. Berkeley: U of California P, 1983.

Roper, Alan. *Arnold's Poetic Landscapes*. Baltimore: Johns Hopkins UP, 1969.

Ruskin, John. *Works*. Vol. 7. London, 1887.

Speller, John L. "Arnold and Immortality." *Arnoldian* 10.2 (1983): 21–25.

Stange, G. Robert. *Matthew Arnold: The Poet as Humanist*. Princeton: Princeton UP, 1967.

Swinburne, A. G. "Matthew Arnold." *Matthew Arnold, the Poetry— The Critical Heritage*. Ed. Carl Dawson. London: Routledge & Kegan Paul, 1973. 168–69.

Trilling, Lionel. *Matthew Arnold*. New York: Harcourt Brace, 1939.

Wilton, Andrew. *Turner and the Sublime*. London: British Museum Publications, 1980.

Chapter 3

Böll, Heinrich. *Billiards at Half-Past Nine*. New York: McGraw-Hill, 1962.

Crawford, John W. "The Utopian Dream, Alive and Well." *Cuyahoga Review*. 1984 Spring–Summer 2 (1): 27–33.

Emerson, Ralph Waldo. *Nature Addresses and Lectures*. Boston: Houghton Mifflin, 1904.

Fitzgerald, F. Scott. *The Great Gatsby*. New York: Scribner's, 1925.

Forster, E. M. *Two Cheers for Democracy*. London: Edward Arnold, 1949.

Heck, Francis S. "The Domain as a Symbol of a Paradise Lost: *Lost Horizon* and *Brideshead Revisited*." *Nassau Review* 4(3): 24–29.

Hilton, James. *Lost Horizon*. New York: William Morrow, 1934.

Mill, John Stuart. *On Liberty*. Ed. Elizabeth Rapaport. New York: Hackett, 1978.

Niebuhr, Reinhold. *The Self and the Dramas of History*. New York: Scribner's, 1955.

Novak, Barbara. "On Defining Luminism." *American Light: The Luminist Movement*. Ed. John Wilmerding. Washington: National Gallery of Art, 1980.

Poulet, Georges. *Studies in Human Time*. Trans. Elliott Coleman. Baltimore: Johns Hopkins UP, 1956.

Chapter 4

Alt, Peter-Andre. *Ironie und Krise*. Frankfurt am Main: Peter Lang, 1985.

Baumgart, Reinhart. *Das Ironische und die Ironie in den Werken Thomas Manns*. München: 1966.

Berendsohn, Walter E. *Thomas Mann—Artist and Partisan in Troubled Times*. Trans. G. C. Buck. University, Alabama: U of Alabama P, 1973.

Borchers, Klaus. *Mythos und Gnosis im Werk Thomas Manns.* Freiburg: Hochschulverlag, 1980.

Brennan, Joseph G. *Thomas Mann's World.* New York: Columbia UP, 1942.

Daemmrich, Horst S. and Ingrid G. Daemmrich. *Spirals and Circles.* 2 vols. New York: Peter Lang, 1994.

Dittman, Ulrich. *Sprachbewusstsein und Redeformen im Werk Thomas Manns.* Stuttgart: W. Kohlhammer Verlag, 1969.

Gronicka, Andre von. *Thomas Mann: Profile and Perspectives.* New York: Random House, 1970.

Hamburger, Käte. *Thomas Manns Biblisches Werk.* München: Nymphenburger Verlagshandlung, 1981.

Hamilton, Nigel. *The Brothers Mann.* New Haven: Yale UP, 1979.

Hatfield, Henry. *Thomas Mann.* Norfolk, Conn.: New Directions, 1951.

————, ed. *Thomas Mann: A Collection of Critical Essays.* Englewood Cliffs, N.J.: Prentice-Hall, 1964.

Heller, Erich. *Thomas Mann—Der ironische Deutsche.* Frankfurt am Main: Suhrkamp Verlag, 1959.

Hoffmann, Gisela E. *Das Motiv des Auserwählten bei Thomas Mann.* Bonn: Bouvier Verlag Herbert Grundmann, 1974.

Hollingdale, R. J. *Thomas Mann—A Critical Study.* London: Rupert Hart-Davis, 1971.

Karthaus, Ulrich. "Der Zauberberg—ein Zeitroman." *Deutsche Vierteljahrsschrift* 44 (1970).

Kaufmann, Fritz. *Thomas Mann—The World as Will and Representation.* Boston: Beacon P, 1957.

Kenosian, David. *Puzzles of the Body. The Labyrinth in Mann's 'Zauberberg,' Kafka's 'Prozess,' and Hesse's 'Steppenwolf.'* New York: Peter Lang, 1995.

Kontje, Todd. *The German Bildungsroman: History of a National Genre.* Columbia, SC: Camden House, 1993.

Koopmann, Helmut. *Die Entwicklung des 'Intellektualen Romans' bei Thomas Mann*. Bonn: Bouvier Verlag Herbert Grundmann, 1971.

————. Thomas Mann. Göttingen: Vandenhoeck & Ruprecht, 1975.

Lange, Victor, ed. *Thomas Mann*. Princeton: Princeton UP, 1975.

Lehnert, Herbert. *Thomas Mann: Fiktion, Mythos, Religion*. Stuttgart: W. Kohlhammer Verlag, 1976.

Mann, Thomas. *The Magic Mountain*. Trans. H. Lowe-Porter. New York: Alfred A. Knopf, 1961.

Pritzlaff, Christiane. *Zahlensymbolik bei Thomas Mann*. Hamburg: Helmut Buske Verlag, 1972.

Rothenberg, Klaus-Jürgen. *Das Problem des Realismus bei Thomas Mann*. Köln: Böhlau Verlag, 1969.

Sandt, Lotti. *Mythos und Symbolik im Zauberberg von Thomas Mann*. Bern: Verlag Paul Haupt, 1979.

Sartre, Jean-Paul. *Existentialism and Humanism*. Trans. Philip Mairet. London: Methuen, 1946.

Saueressig, Heinz. *Die Entstehung des Romans 'Der Zauberberg.'* Biberach an der Riss: 1965.

Scharfschwerdt, Jürgen. *Thomas Mann und der deutsche Bildungsroman*. Stuttgart: W. Kohlhammer Verlag, 1967.

Seidlin, Oskar. Von *Goethe zu Thomas Mann*. Göttingen: 1963.

Swales, Martin. *The German Bildungsroman from Wieland to Hesse*. Princeton, NJ: Princeton, UP, 1978.

Weigand, Hermann J. *The Magic Mountain*. Chapel Hill: U of North Carolina P, 1964.

Williams, C. E. "Not an Inn, But an Hospital." *Thomas Mann's 'The Magic Mountain.'* Ed. Harold Bloom. New York: Chelsea House, 1986. 37–52.

Ziolkowski, Theodore. *Dimensions of the Modern Novel*. Princeton: Princeton UP, 1969.

Conclusion

Burnet, Thomas. *The Theory of the Earth*. London, 1684–90.

Campbell, Joseph. *The Inner Reaches of Outer Space*. New York: Harper & Row, 1986.

Heller, Erich. Thomas *Mann—Der ironische Deutsche*. Frankfurt am Main: Suhrkamp Verlag, 1959.

Perkins, David, ed. *English Romantic Writers*. San Diego: Harcourt Brace, 1967.

Poulet, Georges. *Studies in Human Time*. Trans. Elliott Coleman. Baltimore: Johns Hopkins UP, 1956.

Shaw, Philip. "Romantic Space: Topo-analysis and Subjectivity in *The Prelude*." *Wordsworth's The Prelude*. Ed. Nigel Wood. Buckingham: Open UP, 1993. 75–94.

Thomson, James. *The Seasons*. Ed. James Sambrook. Oxford: Clarendon P, 1981.

Wordsworth, Jonathan, et al. *Wordsworth and the Age of English Romanticism*. New Brunswick, NJ: Rutgers UP, 1987.

Index

Index 171

Studies on Themes and Motifs in Literature

The series is designed to advance the publication of research pertaining to themes and motifs in literature. The studies cover cross-cultural patterns as well as the entire range of national literatures. They trace the development and use of themes and motifs over extended periods, elucidate the significance of specific themes or motifs for the formation of period styles, and analyze the unique structural function of themes and motifs. By examining themes or motifs in the work of an author or period, the studies point to the impulses authors received from literary tradition, the choices made, and the creative transformation of the cultural heritage. The series will include publications of colloquia and theoretical studies that contribute to a greater understanding of literature.

For additional information about this series or for the submission of manuscripts, please contact:

Peter Lang Publishing
Acquisitions Dept.
516 N. Charles St., 2nd Floor
Baltimore, MD 21201